THE EXOTIC KITCHENS OF PERU

CAMINA EL AVTOR

The author (Copeland Marks) travels.

THE EXOTIC KITCHENS OF PERU

The Land of the Inca

Copeland Marks

M. Evans and Company, Inc.

New York

M. Evans and Company, Inc.
216 East 49th Street
New York, New York 10017

ISBN 0-87131-880-6

Designed and typeset by Annemarie Redmond

Manufactured in the United States of America

9 8 7 6 5 4 3 2

CONTENTS

Acknowledgments vii

Foreword xi

Introduction 1

Glossary 7

Tamales, Appetizers, and other Snacks . . . 13

Soups 33

Seafood of all Kinds 59

Beef, Pork, Lamb, and Other Meats . . 107

Chicken, Duck, and Other Poultry 159

Sauces, Salads, and Vegetable Dishes . . 203

Desserts and Beverages 237

Index 261

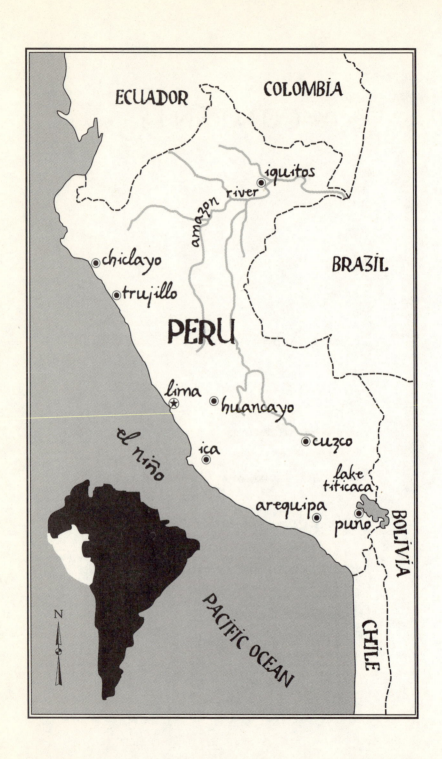

ACKNOWLEDGMENTS

Peru is the third largest country in South America, with abrupt changes in altitude, temperature, rainfall, and all the other physical attributes of a mountainous country. My culinary research, for example, took me from the tropical Amazon region to the brisk altitude of Cuzco (at 10,000 feet elevation) in an hour. Wherever I traveled, cooked, tasted, and recorded, the people of Peru in all of the regions were with me, assisting my project. For this I thank them all and record below the names of the many people who offered me the knowledge of their traditions, sources of inspiration, and cookstove:

Chef Ramiro Vasquez—Lima

Isabel Alvarez—Lima

Marleny Garcia Campos—Trujillo

Luis Sanez—Trujillo

Leonor Rivera de Soto—Trujillo

Luis Alvarez Garcia—Huanchaco

Aldo Ganoza Carbajal—Huanchaco

Florencia Lopez Galvez, Circuito del Pato—Trujillo

Lidia Jaime Araujo—Lambayeque

Isabel Arauja Jaime—Lambayeque

Monica Monsalve Puente—Lambayeque

Isabel Senador—Chiclayo

Esther Curto Cordova—Iquitos

Rolfo Walter Sanches Davila—Iquitos

Sandra Chaves Huaman—Iquitos

Cecilia Kalinowski Venero—Cuzco

Maria Elena Barrionuero—Cuzco

Chef Juan Poma Arocotipa—Puno

Chef Basilio Mami Tinta—Arequipa

Irma Alpaca Polomina—Arequipa

Roberto Ortiz—Arequipa

Juana Gamiro Belledo—Arequipa

Charles Stone, Editor, *Rumbos* Magazine—Lima

My special *saludos* to Ambassador Carlos M. Gamarra Mujica, Consulate General of Peru, Paterson, N.J., and Ana Iglesias whose assistance has been extremely valuable.

Also, Consul General Fernando Rojas, Consulate General of Peru, New York, and the admirable Lola Salas who gave me invaluable information for my trip to Peru and afterward.

Aero Peru outlined my itinerary to Peru and assisted me within the country.

Special mention must be made to Gail Martin of the Gail Martin Gallery, New York, who gave me spectacular slides of the famous antique Peruvian textiles for reproduction in this book.

I appreciate the Americas Society, Park Avenue, New York, for the generous use of their library.

Special mention must be accorded in the New York area to Chef Rodolfo Islas whose knowledge of Callao, Port of Lima, was impressive. Rita Escate Torres helped me considerably with the foods of the Negro community in Chincha.

Victor Yamashiro, Peruvian Family Restaurant, Passaic, NJ, awakened my interest in Peruvian/Japanese cooking. Norma Moromisato contributed to my knowledge of Peruvian/Japanese food. Clara Choy de Vera, Paterson, NJ, expanded my knowledge of Peruvian/Chinese cooking. Angel Miguel Silva, Passaic, NJ, was generous with his time and effort.

Important sources of supply in the United States of the unique Peruvian chili are as follows:

J. Austin Kerr
Peruvian Aji Collection
P.O. Box 281525
San Francisco, CA 94128
and
Old Southwest Trading Company
P.O. Box 7545
Albuquerque, NM 87194

In addition, there are a number of small Peruvian groceries in the New York/New Jersey area, where a variety of Peruvian foods can be found.

My thanks to Jorge Reinoso, Director, Centro de Investigación de Recursos Naturales y Media Ambiente, Puno-Lake Titicaca for providing statistics and other information regarding the potato.

The illustrations in this book are seventeenth century drawings by Guaman Poma de Ayala, a Peruvian prince. The original manuscript of more than 1100 pages is in the Old Royal Collection, National Library of Copenhagen, Denmark. Thanks to the National Library Cuzco, Peru for help in obtaining these drawings.

FOREWORD

After the Spanish conquest destroyed the great Inca Empire of Peru, a new cuisine *criollo* developed, a subtle blending of the cooking of Spain and Peru using the ingredients of old and new worlds. Copeland Marks covers this aspect of the cuisine brilliantly and in depth but goes much further, documenting the influence of immigrants, Chinese and Italian among them, as well as those of African slaves brought in by Spain. Regional kitchens are explored and explained, and the importance of the foods that the Spanish found when Pizarro invaded—notably the potato, which was cultivated in many varieties and which is of inestimable importance in the world today. Though the capsicum family is believed to have originated in Mexico in North America, the Inca, who were among the earliest peoples to have developed agriculture, created their own capsicum varieties. One of them, *Capsicum baccatum,* variety *pendulum Kellu-uchu,* is a most brilliant yellow, an echo of the sun worship of the original Peruvians. It is extremely hot. They are believed to have invented peanut butter and corn differing from the Mexican original that gave birth to popcorn. They probably invented freeze drying, preserving the potato crop in the high Andes. It goes on and on and now, at long last, knowledge of it is available in *The Exotic Kitchens of Peru* brought to us by an author, Copeland Marks, who is greatly esteemed for his work on exotic and little-known kitchens throughout the world. I am grateful to him and his publisher, George de Kay, for giving us this valuable insight into an important area of cookery.

Elisabeth Lambert Ortiz, author of *The Complete Book of Mexican Cooking,* now in a revised edition, *The Complete Book of Latin American Cooking, The Complete Book of Caribbean Cooking,* and *The Complete Book of Japanese Cooking.*

CONQVISTA
GVAINACAPAC, CADIA
INGA   ESPAÑA

INTRODUCTION

From 1531 to 1533 the Spaniard Francisco Pizarro conquered and destroyed the great Inca Empire of Peru.

It was this catastrophic disaster that launched the beginnings of the new culinary outlook in Peru, the cross-cultural exchange of the foods of Europe with what the Spanish found in the new country. In addition, it was also the beginning of the new race—the creoles—the interracial combination of the indigenous peoples of Peru and the Spanish conquerors. There is a dual Inca-Spanish legacy that remains active even in this modern era. (One of the results was the celebrated creole *(criollo)* style of cooking, in natural pottery pots over wood fires, a style that is still exemplified in the *picanterias* of the city of Arequipa.) And there were other arrivals as well. In the middle of the nineteenth century African slaves and Chinese laborers were imported to work in agriculture and in Peru's mines.

The three characteristic Inca foods are *quinoa*, the tiny high-protein grain; corn; and potatoes. To these must be added the *aji*, a botanical group of hot chilies that varies in color but is predominantly orange/gold with various intensities of heat, that are used in one form or another. These four vegetables are of pre-Inca origin and define the pre- and post-Conquest cooking.

And so, over the centuries the ingredients and ways of preparing them became codified into recipes that became known throughout Peru. In this book, each recipe is identified

1

by the name of the specific city or town from which the combination emanated. The city also denotes the regional culinary characteristics. In other words, the cooking of Trujillo, a city in the north, has its own style and way of seasoning, which differs from Lima, the capital city, with its more modern trends in cooking. In addition, Iquitos, on the Amazon River, has its own culinary style that is distinct from all other regions.

Potatoes have been cultivated in Peru for an estimated 6,000 years in the high-altitude areas of Lake Titicaca. On a walk through the public market in Puno, the large city on the shores of the lake, one finds a diversified variety of potatoes in a startling number of sizes, shapes, and colors. There are an estimated forty-eight varieties of potatoes in the Puno-Lake Titicaca region. On display are long-twisted forms, rose-colored knobby shapes, smooth-skinned varieties, and light-brown conventional types. Among them is the yellow potato, which

might be the most desirable of all, with its mealy texture and pleasant flavor. Peruvians admire yellow potatoes very much.

Potatoes are one of the four most important foods in the world. The others are rice, wheat, and corn. Statistics indicate that in 1970 Peruvians consumed 180 kilos (about 360 pounds) of potatoes per person per year. In 1996, consumption had decreased to 45 kilos (about 90 pounds), which is still a considerable quantity.

Nature has been generous to Peru. Everything seems to be available in the vegetable- and fruit-filled markets. The varied climate in the coastal (Lima), Andean (Cuzco), and jungle (Iquitos) regions makes it possible to find all one needs. An adjunct is the cross-cultural culinary contribution of the indigenous people, plus the Chinese, Negro, Japanese, and Italian immigrants. The sheer quantity and diversity of the culinary output is impressive. One can move from city to city

or region to region and find dishes that are characteristic of the area. It makes for an exciting illustration of cooking, tasting, and recording.

When one thinks about the food of Peru, what leaps immediately to mind is *ceviche*, the raw seafood appetizer that is marinated in lemon or lime juice, which cooks it without flame. Red onion, chilies, and cilantro are typically added, but even so, Peruvian *ceviche* will differ from one region to another. The only limiting factor—and it is not one in Peru—is the freshness of the fish, which is derived from the unique and incredibly plentiful waters off the western coast of Peru. The best *ceviche* in all of Central and South America is Peruvian *ceviche*.

Peru probably has the most important cuisine in South America. Historically it combines the indigenous agricultural products of the tribal groups with the middle period, which

saw the introduction of the Chinese and Negro immigrants, and secondarily the Italian immigrants, each of which made its respective culinary contribution. The contemporary (modern) scene is exemplified by the modifications that have occurred in the home kitchens and the attempt by home cooks (and restaurant chefs) to include specialty ingredients from imported sources. It is time that the richness of the Peruvian way of cooking be better known and better appreciated than it is at present.

This book will open a window on the culinary achievements of the Peruvians.

POBRE DE LOS IÑS
DE SEIS ANIMALES QCO

me q tememen. los pobres delos yñs enes te reyno —

corregi-
dor sierpe

amallapallay que
llatana uaycho
por amor de
dios rayco

tigre-
espanoles deltabo

leon
comendero

zorra
p dela dotrina

gato
escriuano

rraton
caciq principal

estos dhos animales q
no temen adios desuella
alos pobres delos yñs
enes te reyno y no ay
remedio

pobre de jesucristo   q ue los

GLOSSARY

***Achiote* (also called annatto [*Bixa orellana*])** is a red/orange vegetable coloring without much flavor that derives from the seeds of the annatto tree. Achiote can be purchased in paste or granules. If you purchase the granules, they must be first dissolved in hot corn oil before being used in a recipe.

***Aji (capsicum, baccatum* species)** is the distinctive hot chili grown in Peru that is indispensable in any traditional cooking of the country. *Ajis* differ in size, shape, and heat intensity. The following list describes this chili:

Aji Varieties
Each *aji* has its own distinct taste!

Aji Amarillo/Escabeche, also known in the U.S. as yellow chili or yellow Peruvian chili, are the most common ajis in Peru. They are 4 to 6 inches in length and a deep orange color when ripe. Grown in all regions of the country, they are eaten almost daily in Peru in sauces and seasonings. Their heat value is moderate (40 to 50 thousand Scoville units). Available in powder and dried whole form. *Aji Amarillo* is also available in pickled form, packed in large 12-ounce jars. *Author's Note: Aji Amarillo* are available in cans as well and are sold at local Peruvian markets.

Red Aji Limo* and *Yellow Aji Limo originate from the northern coast of Peru. The pods are small, round, and belly-shaped—about 1½ to 3 inches long—and ripen into a deep red, yellow, or orange color. Peruvians tend to eat *Aji Limo* during the cold winter season, particularly in seafood dishes, because it stores well and is very hot (50 to 60 thousand Scoville units). Available in powder and dried whole.

7

Aji Cereza is a variety very similar to the cherry chili pepper (*Cereza* translates to "cherry"). *Aji Cereza* is found in the Peruvian jungle but is only sold at local town markets. They are deep red in color when ripe, round, and very small—about 1 inches in diameter. Available in pickled form only.

Aji Charapa is a wild variety found near the city of Iquitos. Red and yellow in color, *Aji Charapa* are very small, with a diameter of less than ½ inch. Very hot! Available in pickled form only.

Aji Verde is found mainly in northern Peru, near Lambayeque and Piura. Though the name translates to "green *aji*," they are yellow, orange, and red in color. They are 1 to 1½ inches in length and considerably hot. Available in pickled form only.

Aji Mono translates to "monkey *aji*." It is a regional variety grown in the Peruvian jungle. When ripe, *Aji Mono* turn bright red and are 3 to 5 inches long. *Aji Mono* is representative of the diet eaten by jungle dwellers because it is extremely hot. Available in pickled forms only and packed in larger 12-ounce jars to accommodate their length.

Aji Pinguita de Mono, a smaller version of *Aji Mono,* is among the hottest *ajis* in Peru! They also are bright red in color but only about 1 inch long. Aji Pinguita de Mono are found mainly in the central valley of Chanchamayo. Available in pickled forms only.

—Contributed by J. Austin Kerr, Peruvian *Aji* Collection.

Cassava (Manthot utilissima) is called tapioca in some places. In Peru, it is known as yuca. See Yuca.

Cherimoya (also known as custard apple [Anonacac family]) is a remarkable tropical fruit about the size of a large grapefruit, with a scaly outer surface and a creamy, luscious pulp scattered throughout with smooth large black seeds. The botanical origin is tropical Central/South America. Cherimoya was introduced into India in the sixteenth century, possibly by the Portuguese, and for some time was thought to have originated in that country, which is where I first tasted it. Not so. Its origin is Central/South America, and I have enjoyed its unrivaled flavor not only in Peru but also in Guatemala.

Chuno are freeze-dried whole potatoes that can be seen in public markets in Peru. They look like the white round stones one finds on a beach. The potatoes are 2 to 3 inches in length, are hard, and take some cooking to be edible. They are available here in Peruvian markets. Grown in the wind-swept, treeless altiplano, the Andean highlands in the vicinity of Lake Titicaca, they are part of the diet of the inhabitants of the Andean highlands.

Cuy (guinea pig) was originally considered a rodent, but has achieved Nirvana by recently being scientifically placed in another biological category. Hopefully, this change in status will make it less off-putting as a food. In Peru, the animal is domesticated, and it is a common sight to find them, tail-less and furry, scurrying around homes. In markets, they are ready for the cooking pan, where they are typically used in stews or deep fried. Peruvians like *cuy* very much and reserve it for auspicious occasions, not an everyday dish.

Huacatay (Marigold Tagetes Minutae J.) is a flowering member of the marigold family that is used in Peru as a seasoning in cooking as well as for medicinal purposes. One report about *huacatay* states that bunches of the flowers are hung in houses to keep out bats. An annual, it grows to about 3 feet in height. Chopped fresh and dried *huacatay* has a light, pleasant marigold floral aroma. Recipes that call for this esoteric herb are included in this book.

Papa Seca is another form of freeze-dried potatoes that have been cut into ¼-inch cubes, then left to dry into small hard bits in the high altitudes of Peru. These potatoes must be reconstituted—soaked in water—before being used in a recipe. They are available here in Peruvian markets.

Picanteria was originally a local bar where one could have a meal and drink large amounts of the delicious fermented homemade drink called *chicha*. The several such establishments that I saw in Cuzco were dark and dingy and looked like nothing better than dens of iniquity, but they were not rowdy.

The most attractive and modern *picanterias* are in the city of Arequipa, where they have large sheds for dining indoors and spacious outdoor seating in colorful gardens. An impressive number of traditional foods cooked over wood-burning fires in the kitchens of *picanterias* constitute some of the best food in all of Peru.

Queso Fresco is firmly packed, fresh cheese that is chalk white in color. It has a neutral flavor because it is not aged. When it is not available in Peruvian or Latin American food markets, substitute Feta cheese. (Remember, however, that Feta is salted.) If you are making the famous dish Papa a la Huancaina (page 226), take the time to secure *queso fresco.*

Quinoa (Amaranthacono family) is a wonderful grain that is eaten in the highlands of Peru and was used by the Incas before the Spanish Conquest. It contains 12 to 22 percent protein. The small grains look very much like toasted sesame seeds and are cooked in soups and other combinations, including beverages, in Peru. *Quinoa* becomes translucent after being cooked.

Yuca is a popular vegetable in Peru. The large woody-looking roots are the edible parts and must be peeled before being cooked. Yuca is available in Hispanic markets and supermarkets. It makes excellent French fries. Do not confuse yuca with yucca (note the two c's), which is an ornamental plant found in the western United States.

Zapallo (probably *Curbita moschata*) is the giant hard-shelled calabaza, or squash, the botanical origin of which is Peru. To see a heap of these squash in the public markets is an astonishing sight. One is larger than another, weighing twenty to thirty pounds. Slices of this attractive orange-colored vegetable are sold freshly cut in the markets. A reasonable substitute here is butternut squash.

CHACASVIOIOGACOSIVGA

GVAMBOCHACA

uedor de puentes   puentes

TAMALES, APPETIZERS, AND OTHER SNACKS

This chapter could also be called Endangered Species, since the recipes that follow are labor-intensive, and each year fewer ethnic cooks wish to make tamales, for example, as their mothers did. The excuse is always too much work. Yet, to allow any of the recipes in this group to be lost to the electronic shortcuts of the Twentieth Century would be an insult to the dedicated cook.

This should not serve to intimidate any who wish to make the more complicated dishes, like the excellent Saltena de Pollo (Chicken and Vegetable Pies), but to encourage them. Appetizers and snacks fill an important and useful category in Peruvian cooking. Moreover, most of them can be prepared, then cooled and frozen, which is an enormous advantage and eliminates frequent cooking and assembly.

I urge the reader who is interested in the ethnic cooking of Peru to make the effort and, in essence, save the old-time preparations from extinction. Nothing ventured, nothing gained.

Tamales Especiales (Trujillo)

CLASSIC PERUVIAN TAMALES

A number of Latin American countries prepare noted tamales of different sizes, shapes, and ingredients: Mexico, Guatemala, Nicaragua, Ecuador, and, of course, Peru. They all have one thing in common—masa harina, which is cornmeal ground purposely for use in tamales. It is the additional ingredients in any tamales that give them their character.

THE MAZA

2   pounds *masa harina* (about 8 cups)

2   tablespoons chopped, seeded fresh *aji amarillo* (yellow Peruvian chili, see Glossary)

1   tablespoon salt, or more to taste

2   teaspoons *achiote* granules (see Glossary), dissolved in 4 teaspoons hot corn oil

½   cup corn oil

11 to 12 cups hot water, depending upon the firmness of the mix

In a large bowl mix the *masa harina, aji,* salt, *achiote* oil, corn oil, and hot water, adding it a little at a time, stirring as you go, until combined well; set aside.

THE STUFFING

¼   cup corn oil

5   cloves garlic, ground to a paste with 3 tablespoons water

1   pound skinless chicken breast, cut into thumb-sized pieces

10   scallions, trimmed and sliced

3   teaspoons dried yellow *aji* chili powder (see Glossary)

1   teaspoon pepper

1   teaspoon cumin

Heat the oil in a skillet. Stir in the garlic paste, then add the chicken and stir-fry over low heat for 2 minutes. Add the scallions, *aji* powder, pepper, and cumin, and stir-fry for 5 minutes; set aside to cool.

PREPARE THE TAMALES

3   **hard-boiled eggs, peeled and each cut lengthwise into 8 slices**

25   **black olives, pitted (one for each tamale)**

60   **dried corn leaves**

     Nylon thread or raffia (*hunco*)

1. On the work surface spread out 2 corn leaves, placing one halfway over the other. Place ½ cup of the cornmeal mash in the center of the 2 overlapping leaves. Press the mash down into a rectangle 1 inch thick and 4 to 5 inches long. Make a depression in the mash and add 2 tablespoons chicken stuffing. Place 1 olive on one end and 1 slice of egg on the other. Fold one leaf over toward the center and the other leaf over that.

2. Using nylon thread or raffia, tie one end of the tamale, about 2 inches from the end. Turn the tamale and tie the other end. Now wrap the tamale lengthwise with the thread.

3. Make the tamales, filling and tying them with the remaining leaves and stuffing, in the same way.

4. Place the tied tamales in a large pan and add hot water to come up to just the top of the tamales. Cover the pan, bring the water to a boil over moderate/low heat, and cook for 1½ to 2 hours.

Serve warm. **Makes about 25 tamales**

Note: Cooked tamales can be frozen. Cool well, then store in plastic bags, and freeze. When ready to use, let them thaw for 1 or 2 hours. Place in 1 to 2 inches of boiling water and cook for 10 minutes.

    Aluminum foil, light or medium weight, can be used instead of the traditional dried corn leaves. For each tamale, cut a sheet of foil 12 inches square. Place ½ cup of the cornmeal mash in the center of the foil sheet. Follow the same instructions above for filling. Fold one long side of the foil toward the center; fold the other long side over it. Fold each short end into a triangle and fold into the middle. It should be tightly wrapped. The package may also be tied up or not, as you wish. In any event, make a tight package, wrapping the foil as you would giftwrap a box.

Humitas (Chiclayo)

STEAMED WHOLE CORN KERNEL TAMALES

Humitas are really the classic tamales, just in a different guise. The ingredients here are different, but the technique of stuffing the dried corn leaves (available in any Mexican food market), tying them into tight bundles, and boiling them in water (for only 20 minutes) is the same.

THE CORN

4	cups (2 pounds) fresh or thawed frozen corn niblets (kernels)
1	tablespoon corn oil
1	teaspoon *achiote* granules (see Glossary), dissolved in 2 teaspoons hot corn oil
1	teaspoon salt
⅛	teaspoon pepper

1. In a food processor process the corn niblets into a mush with some texture. (It should not be smooth.) Transfer to a bowl and stir in the oil, *achiote*, salt, and pepper; set aside for ½ hour to thicken.

THE HUMITAS

About 25 dried corn leaves

1	fresh *aji amarillo* (yellow Peruvian chili, see Glossary) seeded, and cut into 10 julienne slices
10	black olives, pitted and halved
1	small onion, sliced thin (⅓ cup)
¼	teaspoon achiote granules, dissolved in 1 teaspoon hot corn oil

- ¼ teaspoon salt
- 1 pound skinless chicken breast, cut into 10 thumb-sized pieces
- 2 hard-boiled eggs, peeled and each cut lengthwise into 10 slices

1. Arrange 2 corn leaves as slices as instructed Tamales Especiales (see preceding recipe). Take 2 generous tablespoons of the corn niblet mush and place it in the center of the corn leaves.

2. In a small skillet stir-fry the *aji*, black olives, onion, *achiote* oil, and ¼ teaspoon salt over low heat for 2 minutes. Remove and cool.

3. Make a depression in the corn mush and add 1 piece of chicken and 1 slice of egg. From the stir-fried mixture add 1 slice of *aji*, 2 halves of black olives, and a few slices of onion. Cover with 2 tablespoons more of the corn mush, pressing it down into a rectangle. Fold the corn leaves over, and tie the tamale as indicated on page 15. Form tamales with the remaining ingredients and corn leaves and tie them in the same way. Boil in hot water following the directions on page 15 for 20 minutes. Drain.

Upon serving, unfold the *humitas* and serve warm. **Makes 10**

Juane de Yuca (Iquitos)
YUCA PACKAGES

Juane is a traditional food, a differently shaped tamale of the Amazonian city of Iquitos and is sold in public markets all tied up ready to go in its characteristic round pouch shape. Yuca root is grated and seasoned, topped with a piece of fish, and boiled in water for an hour. In Iquitos, these are not wrapped in aluminum foil, which is what I have used here. There they are prepared with bijau, a flexible jungle leaf that is filled, then firmly tied up with a kind of rattan thread—some things we would find difficult to duplicate here.

4	pounds yuca (see Glossary), peeled and rinsed in cold water
4	tablespoons corn oil
I	cup chopped sweet red pepper
I	teaspoon cumin
I	teaspoon salt, or to taste
3	cloves garlic, chopped fine
6	sprigs fresh cilantro processed to a paste with 2 tablespoons water
I	pound fish fillet, such as flounder or similar fish, cut into 8 to 10 pieces, one for each package
8	to 10 squares (12 inches) aluminum foil

1. Grate the yuca on the fine side of a hand grater or in a food processor. Transfer to a bowl and stir in 2 tablespoons of the oil until combined.

2. Heat the remaining 2 tablespoons of oil in a skillet. Add the red pepper, cumin, salt, and garlic and stir-fry over low heat for 3 minutes. Add to the yuca with the cilantro paste and mix well.

3. Put ½ cup of the yuca mixture in the center of 1 sheet of the foil squares. Top with 1 piece of fish and cover it with another ½ cup of the yuca mixture.

4. Fold the 4 corners of the foil toward the center. Twist the corners firmly to seal the package into a rounded pouch shape. Prepare with the remaining filling and foil in the same way. Put the packages, standing upright, side by side, in a saucepan. Add enough water to the pan to come at least halfway up the sides of the packages. Bring the water to a boil, cover, and cook over low heat for 1 hour.

Unwrap and serve warm. **Makes 8 to 10**

Juane de Arroz (Iquitos)

RICE PACKAGES

Like Juane de Yuca (preceding recipe), the rice package is jungle food, a meal to be carried when traveling or eaten at home in the Amazonian region. These packages are available for sale in public markets, but all of the home cooks I met in the city of Iquitos prepared them for their families.

2	tablespoons corn oil
2	cloves garlic, chopped
½	teaspoon turmeric
3	cups rice, well rinsed, soaked in water to cover ½ hour, cooked until *al dente*, and cooled
3	eggs, beaten
1	teaspoon salt, or to taste
12	squares (12 inches) aluminum foil
8	pieces boneless hen, light or dark meat, 3 inches long by 1 inch wide
8	black olives, pitted
2	hard-boiled eggs, peeled and quartered

1. Heat the oil in a skillet and stir-fry the garlic and turmeric over low heat for 1 minute.

2. Put the rice in a large bowl and add the garlic mixture. Stir in the beaten eggs and salt.

3. Put ¾ cup of the cooked rice mixture in the middle of 1 foil square. Push into the rice piece of hen, 1 olive, and 1 egg quarter. Cover with ½ cup of the rice mixture.

4. Fold the 4 corners of the foil toward the center. Twist the corners firmly to seal the package to prevent water from entering. Prepare packages with the remaining ingredients and foil in the same way.

5. Put the 8 bundles standing upright, side by side, in a saucepan. Add

enough water to the pan to come at least halfway up the sides of the packages. Bring to a boil and cook over low heat for ½ hour.

Unwrap and serve warm. **Makes 8 packages**

Ocopa Arequipena (Arequipa)
OCOPA FROM AREQUIPA

I cannot translate ocopa, *except to say that it is a popular appetizer from the beautiful city of Arequipa and is nationally known and appreciated in Peru. It incorporates evaporated milk, fresh cheese,* huacatay, *ground peanuts, all of which is then thickened with crushed cookies. These idiosyncratic ingredients help describe the popularity of* ocopa.

1	tablespoon corn oil
1	sweet green pepper, cut into 1-inch pieces (¾ cup)
1	medium onion, quartered (½ cup)
1	tablespoon *huacatay* (see Glossary)
1	teaspoon salt, or to taste
2	tablespoons dry roasted peanuts, ground fine
1	cup evaporated milk
½	cup coarsely mashed *queso fresco* (see Glossary) or Feta cheese
3	sweet vanilla cookies, crushed (see Note)
	lettuce leaves, for serving
4	potatoes (1¼ pounds), cooked in their skins, peeled and sliced lengthwise
	tomato slices, for serving
2	hard-boiled eggs, peeled and quartered
6	black olives, pitted

1. Heat the oil in a large skillet. Add the green pepper, onion, *huacatay*, salt, and peanuts and stir-fry over low heat for 2 minutes.

2. Transfer the mixture to a food processor and process to a smooth consistency. Add the milk, cheese, and cookies and process again until smooth.

To serve, arrange the lettuce leaves over a serving platter (or individual plates). Place the potatoes in the center. Arrange the tomato slices around the edge of the platter. Pour the cheese sauce over the potatoes, then garnish with the olives and eggs.

Serve at room temperature or cold as an appetizer. **Serves 6**

Note: Some Peruvian recipes contain either plain sweet cookies or tea biscuits or crushed soda crackers (saltines) for the purpose of thickening a sauce. Some cooks prefer to use the small animal crackers, crushed.

Yuca Relleno (Trujillo)

STUFFED YUCA SNACKS

Yuca is now commonly found in markets where there is a Latin American community living. People of the tropics have long eaten the dark-brown-skinned root with its bleached white pulp, as have people in Asia (Malaysia) and Africa. So why not in the United States? There is great variety to the way it can be prepared, from French-fried yuca to sweet and savory preparations like the one that follows.

This recipe may also be prepared with mashed potatoes instead of mashed yuca. The stuffing and assembling as well as the cooking time remain the same.

THE YUCA

2   **pounds yuca (see Glossary), peeled and cut into ½-inch slices**

2   **teaspoons corn oil**

1. In a saucepan cook the yuca in boiling water to cover for 20 minutes. Drain.

2. While the yuca is hot, mash it, removing the hard fibers as you mash along, mixing in the oil. Form the yuca into 6 equal balls and set aside.

THE STUFFING

2	tablespoons corn oil
½	pound ground beef
½	teaspoon salt
¼	teaspoon pepper
¼	teaspoon cumin
¼	teaspoon dried oregano
1	tablespoon raisins
½	cup chopped onion
2	tablespoons chopped tomato
¼	teaspoon paprika
1	tablespoon chopped parsley

Prepare the stuffing: Heat the oil in a large skillet. Add the beef, salt, pepper, cumin, and oregano and stir-fry over moderate heat for 2 minutes. Add the raisins, onion, tomato, paprika, and parsley and mix well. Cover the pan for 2 minutes, then stir-fry a moment to combine; set aside to cool.

THE SNACK

2	hard-boiled eggs, peeled and quartered
1	cup corn oil for deep-frying

1. Take 1 yuca ball and flatten it out somewhat in your palm. Add 1 heaping tablespoon of the stuffing and egg quarter. Close the yuca over the stuffing and shape the ball into an oval football. Repeat with the remaining ingredients.

2. Heat the oil in a wok or large skillet. Add the yuca ovals and deep-fry them over moderate heat, turning, for about 3 minutes. Drain on paper towels.

Serve warm, with rice and salad side dishes. **Serves 6**

Puchucuy de Maiz (Iquitos)

CORNMEAL AND YUCA SNACKS

*This is jungle food, very compelling and habit forming. I was on a
sixty-foot bargelike boat moving down the Amazon River with a random group
of village people. The boat had a canvas and board cover—shelter from the
sun and rain. We moved slowly, stopping to deliver bananas, passengers,
lumber, and a curious tourist. The river was placid, very wide, with an almost
impenetrable jungle on both sides. Yet, small villages did exist near the
shoreline. Surprisingly, there were no wildlife or birds since they are nocturnal.*

*Along the way a village woman came on board with a large basket of these.
They were still warm. They were wonderful!*

2	**pounds yuca (see Glossary), peeled and rinsed in cold water**
1	**pound cornmeal (3½ cups)**
1½	**cups sugar**
1	**teaspoon baking powder**
¼	**cup corn oil**
	8 to 10 squares (8 inches) aluminum foil

1. In a processor grind the yuca until finely chopped. Transfer the yuca to
a large bowl and add the cornmeal. Add the sugar and baking powder and
combine everything well. Set aside for 10 minutes, then stir in the oil.

2. Put ⅛ cup of the mixture in the center of 1 of the foil squares. Press
into a 4 inch long and 1½-inch wide rectangle. Fold both long sides of
the foil over to cover the filling. Then fold each end into a V-shape and
fold them toward the middle to seal the package. Make snacks with
the remaining filling and foil in the same way.

3. Bake the packages in a preheated 350 degree oven for 15 to 20
minutes. Then open the package and test to see if the *puchucuy* is firm
to the touch. If not, refold and bake another 5 minutes.

Serve warm. **Makes 8 to 10**

Saltena de Pollo (Puno)

CHICKEN AND VEGETABLE PIES

Every morning at 9 o'clock, I would leave my hotel in Puno and go looking for an elderly lady who would sit on the cement curb at the central market. She was almost always covered by a black umbrella that shielded her from the intense sunlight. In a nicely decorated handwoven basket, with a clean linen cloth on top, she sold these classic chicken pies that could win a prize anywhere. I would buy two, devouring one immediately and keeping the other for later. The pies sold quickly and one would have to wait until the next day to restock. She never did give me her name.

THE DOUGH

4   cups flour

2   teaspoons salt

2   teaspoons sugar

¼   teaspoon dry yeast

I   cup warm water

½   pound very soft lard or margarine, at room temperature

Put the flour in a large bowl and make a well in the center. Add the salt, sugar, yeast and most of the warm water. Mix lightly, then stir in the soft lard or margarine. Push the flour in from all sides (I prefer a fork to do this) and mix until a soft dough forms. Dust with flour and set aside.

THE STUFFING

I   tablespoon corn oil

I   small onion, chopped (⅓ cup)

⅓   cup chopped tomato

I   teaspoon salt

¼   teaspoon pepper

¼   teaspoon cumin

½   pound boneless chicken breast, cut into thumb-sized pieces

1½   **cups water**

1   **pound carrots, cut into 1/4-inch dice**

½   **cup cooked, diced potatoes**

¼   **cup fresh or frozen green peas**

1. Heat the oil in a large skillet. Add the onion and tomato and stir-fry over low heat for 2 minutes. Add the salt, pepper, cumin, chicken, and water and cook for 2 minutes.

2. Add the carrots and simmer for 5 minutes. Lastly, add the potatoes and peas and cook until soft. Stir gently but well to combine. This is a dry fry and all of the liquid should evaporate. Cool. Remove the chicken pieces and set aside.

THE PIES

1   **egg, beaten**

10   **black olives, pitted**

1. Pull off a chunk of dough and roll it into a ball 2½ inches in diameter.

2. On a lightly floured surface roll the dough into a pancake 5 inches in diameter. In the center put 3 generous tablespoons stuffing, 1 piece of chicken, and 1 olive. Fold over both sides of the dough to meet in the center, then pinch the edges of the sides firmly to enclose the filling. Brush the top with the beaten egg. Place the pie on a lightly oiled baking sheet. Make pies with the remaining dough and stuffing, sealing them in the same way.

3. Bake the pies in a preheated 350 degree oven for 15 minutes, or until light brown.

Serve warm, with lime slices for squeezing over the pies. **Makes 8 or 9**

Variations: Two other stuffings can be used:

1. *Mozzarella Cheese:* Grate coarsely about ½ pound mozzarella and season with ¼ teaspoon pepper. Stuff, seal, and bake the pies as directed above.

2. *Beef:* Leftover roast beef is a good substitute for the chicken, as is any other type of cooked beef. Cut ½ pound cooked beef into ¼-inch cubes. Follow the steps for making the chicken stuffing, except stir in the beef last when you add the potatoes and peas.

Chicharrónes de Pescado (Chincha)
CRISP FISH CUBES

This very popular fish fry can be served as a snack with drinks or as an appetizer preceding a meal. The people of Chincha rely on fish from the nearby Pacific Ocean since it is easily available and economical. The fish is usually served with a simple Zarza (page 214), made with red onion, tomato, salt, pepper, and an ample amount of fresh lemon juice.

Boneless pork cubes may also be prepared this way. Cut the pork into ¾-inch cubes and use the same mixture to coat them as for the fish. The frying time will be longer for pork. Chicharrónes of pork are served for breakfast as well as on other occasions.

3	**pounds fillet of cod, flounder, or similar white-fleshed fish, cut into 1-inch cubes**
4	**cloves garlic, ground to a paste with 2 tablespoons water**
½	**teaspoon salt, or to taste**
⅛	**teaspoon pepper**
1	**teaspoon soy sauce**
1	**cup flour**
1	**cup or more corn oil for deep-frying**
	Zarza (page 204)

1. In a bowl mix all the ingredients, except the oil, together well. There should be enough moisture so that the flour clings to the fish cubes.

2. Heat the oil in a wok or skillet over moderate heat. Fry the fish, a few cubes at a time, for 2 to 3 minutes until crisp. Drain on paper towels.

Serve warm, with the *Zarza*. **Serves 6 to 8**

Chicharrónes de Chancho (Iquitos)
CRISPY PORK CUBES

Everyone likes chicharrónes *in Peru, and in other places, too, such as Mexico and Guatemala. These tidbits make an appealing appetizer, and the cooks of Iquitos on the Amazon River prepare them this way.*

1	**pound pork spareribs (or a boneless pork roast) cut into 2-inch pieces**
1	**teaspoon salt**
½	**teaspoon cumin**
1	**tablespoon fresh lime juice**
1	**teaspoon corn oil**

1. In a bowl mix all the ingredients together, except the oil. Set aside for 15 minutes.

2. Heat the oil in a skillet, add the pork mixture and stir-fry it over low heat turning now and then for about ½ hour, until the meat is crisp and brown and the fat has cooked off.

Drain briefly on paper towels and serve warm, as an appetizer with drinks. **Serves 4 to 6**

Camote Frito (Chincha)

FRENCH-FRIED SWEET POTATOES

*Sweet potatoes, in any form, are popular in Peru and turn up
in several guises. These are sliced into rounds, deep-fried, then served
with* Chicharrónes de Chancho *(page 27).*

**1 to 2 pounds sweet potatoes, each about 2½ inches in
diameter**

Corn oil for deep-frying

1. Peel the sweet potatoes and slice them into rounds ¼ inch thick.

2. Heat enough oil for deep-frying in a wok or large skillet until hot.
Add the sweet potatoes and fry the slices over moderate heat until crisp
and brown, about 3 to 4 minutes. Drain on paper towels and serve with
the *chicharrónes* or as an appetizer with drinks. **Serves 4 or more**

Camote Relleno (Cuzco)

MASHED SWEET POTATO STUFFED WITH CHEESE

*This is a very popular family snack that I had in a friend's home in Cuzco.
And why not? Stuffed with a generous strip of fresh cheese and deep fried,
these can be enjoyed with a cup of good tea or coffee or as an adjunct to a meal.*

2	pounds sweet potatoes
2	eggs
¼	teaspoon salt
⅛	teaspoon pepper
¼	teaspoon baking powder
8	strips mozzarella cheese, each 4 inches long by ½ inch wide
1	cup corn oil for deep-frying

1. Cook the sweet potatoes in water over moderate heat until soft, about 30 minutes. Drain, peel, and mash.

2. Beat the eggs with the salt, pepper, and baking powder. Set aside.

3. Take ½ cup mashed potato and roll it into a ball. Flatten it out in the palm of your hand, insert 1 cheese strip and cover with potato to form a rounded shape 5 inches long and 2 inches wide. Stuff the mashed potatoes with the remaining cheese in the same way.

4. Heat the oil in a wok or skillet. Roll the stuffed sweet potato in the egg and brown over moderate heat on all sides. Brown the stuffed sweet potatoes over moderate heat on all sides. Drain on paper towels.

Serve warm, with Salsa Criolla (page 204) or your favorite *Zarza* (see Index). **Makes 8**

Causa Limena (Lima)
STUFFED MASHED POTATOES

This appetizer, a popular national dish, is from Lima, the capital city of Peru, which has metropolitan and modern ideas. The dictionary does not reveal how the word "causa" came to be applied to a concoction, albeit a delicious one, that features cold mashed potatoes.

A causa *is considered a light lunch or snack, a most appealing dish that is often served at weddings or other celebrations.*

THE MASHED POTATOES

2	pounds potatoes, peeled
3	teaspoons dried yellow *aji* chili powder (see Glossary)
1	teaspoon turmeric
1	teaspoon salt
2	tablespoons corn oil

Cook the whole potatoes in water over moderate heat until soft. Mash until relatively smooth. Process the *aji* chili with 2 tablespoons water, the turmeric, salt, and oil until smooth. Stir the spice paste into the potatoes and mix well.

THE CHICKEN FILLING

1	cup cooked finely chopped light and dark chicken meat
¼	cup finely chopped celery heart
2	sprigs flat-leaf parsley, chopped fine
½	teaspoon salt
½	cup mayonnaise

In a bowl combine all the filling ingredients until smooth.

THE CAUSA

	Oil for the pan
1	cake pan or Pyrex dish, 8 inches long by 4 inches wide
½	teaspoon finely chopped parsley

1. Spread half of the mashed potato in the oiled dish.

2. Spread all of the filling over the potatoes. Cover with the balance of the potatoes. Cover with plastic wrap and chill until cold.

Serve cold, cut into 2-inch-wide slices. **Serves 6**

Note: The filling may also be prepared with cooked shrimp, canned tuna, or sardines. Use the same quantity and seasonings as for the chicken filling.

CAPITVLO PRIMERO ENTIERO DELL̃GA
INCAILLAPA AIADEFV TO

pucullo

yllapa defunto

en tierra

SOUPS

The soups of Peru are an important consideration for the homemaker, since they may be considered an economical factor when it comes to feeding large families. From a culinary point of view, there is a large variety to choose from, since each region has its own specialty, as well as the different communities that contributed to the overall Peruvian cuisine, such as the Negro, Chinese, Japanese, Italian, and indigenous creole population.

There are two types of soup: those that are meat-based, using beef, pork, poultry, kid, and lamb, and those that are seafood-based and are so popular along the coast of Peru, where the Humboldt Current provides an inexhaustible source of fish. The Chupe de Camarones, Shrimp Soup of Lima, is an astonishing example. Parihuela (page 41), a fish and shellfish soup that is Japanese contributed, still reveals its Peruvian origin.

In the Andes highlands, there is a chill in the air at high altitudes and these areas are predictably soup country. Here lamb, beef, and poultry provide a rich broth that is often supplemented by potatoes of several types, quino, whole wheat kernels, and popular vegetables such as peas, squash, carrots, and fava beans. Soups that stick to the ribs for peasant appetites are paramount.

In the tropical Amazon basin, an amazing soup, Inchicapi de Gallina (page 54), is prepared with a large hen, peanuts, cornmeal, and yuca, among other things.

Peruvian soups enrich the table.

Chupe de Canerejo (Santa Rosa)
CRAB SOUP

The freshness of the seafood from the northern ports of Peru
distinguishes the soups that are so popular in that area. Quantity,
quality, and variety are the hallmarks.

2	tablespoons corn oil
5	cloves garlic, ground to a paste
1	medium onion, chopped (½ cup)
1	ripe tomato, chopped (½ cup)
1	teaspoon salt, or to taste
⅛	teaspoon pepper
3	cups water
12	Maryland-style crabs, top shell removed, bottom cut in half
3	cups milk
5	eggs

1. Heat the oil in a large saucepan, add the garlic, onion, tomato, salt, and pepper, and stir-fry over moderate heat for 2 minutes.

2. Add the water, bring to a boil, and add the crabs, both tops and bottoms. Cover the pan and cook for 5 minutes. Add the milk and bring to a boil over low heat. Simmer, uncovered, for 3 minutes.

3. Crack 1 egg into each soup bowl and pour some of the hot broth over it. (The heat of the soup will cook the egg.) Then add crab pieces to each bowl.

Serve hot, in bowls, with 1 egg per person. **Serves 5**

Fish Broth (Peruvian/Japanese)

Preparing seafood is a basic way of life for the Japanese wherever they reside, and a basic fish broth always available when needed is indispensable. Here is the simple and effective way to make it.

20 cups (5 quarts) water
About 5 pounds fish head and bones, rinsed

1. Put the water and fish in a pot large enough to hold them and bring to a boil, skimming off the foam that rises to the surface. Cover the pot and simmer over low heat for ½ hour.

2. Pour the broth through a metal strainer into a large saucepan and discard the fish. Cool the broth, cover, and refrigerate. Keeps up to 1 week.   ;

Makes a generous 16 cups (4 quarts)

Sopa de Choro (Peruvian/Japanese)

GREEN MUSSEL SOUP

The Japanese prefer the green mussels from New Zealand to the black-shelled type because of their flavor and texture. There are so many mussels to be found offshore in the waters of Peru that there is no difficulty in finding them. Green mussels are also available in the New York City area and are sold frozen in the bins of wholesalers. They are also available fresh.

1	tablespoon corn oil
1	tablespoon chopped garlic
16	cups (4 quarts) Fish Broth (previous recipe)
1	cup chopped fresh tomato
1	cup chopped onion
2	teaspoons salt, or to taste
½	teaspoon pepper
3	pounds green mussels (36), well scrubbed in cold water
½	pound dried spaghetti (#8 size), cooked until *al dente* and drained
3	scallions, sliced thin, for garnish

1. Heat the oil in a wok or skillet and stir-fry the garlic over low heat for 1 minute. Add the fish broth and bring to a boil. Add the tomato, onion, salt, pepper, and mussels and simmer over high heat for 5 minutes.

2. Add the spaghetti, stir everything together well, and simmer for 2 minutes. Remove any mussels that have not opened and discard.

Serve hot, garnished with the scallions. **Serves 6 to 8**

Chupe de Camarones (Chiclayo)

SHRIMP SOUP

*Expect an outstanding soup if it is made from the fresh shrimp
found in the waters off the west coast of Peru. It will be characterized by
a rich concentration of flavors and the aroma of the sea.*

1	tablespoon corn oil
¼	cup sliced onion
4	cloves garlic, ground to a paste with 2 tablespoons water
1	teaspoon paprika
½	cup chopped ripe tomato
1½	pounds medium shrimp, peeled and deveined
5	cups Fish Broth (page 35)
½	cup cooked rice
6	eggs (optional but traditional)
¼	teaspoon salt
⅛	teaspoon pepper
1	cup milk
1	teaspoon dried oregano
¼	cup fresh or frozen green peas
1	ear of corn, fresh or frozen, cut into 6 rounds

1. Heat the oil in a wide pan. Add the onion, garlic paste, paprika, and tomato, and stir-fry over low heat for 3 minutes. Add the shrimp and stir-fry for 2 minutes.

2. Add the broth and rice and bring to a boil. Break the eggs, 1 at a time, into the hot soup, add the salt and pepper, and simmer for 2 minutes. Add the milk, oregano, green peas, and corn and cook for 2 minutes more.

Serve hot in bowls with 1 egg per person. **Serves 6**

Chupe de Camarones del Mar (Lima)

SEA SHRIMP SOUP

*Seafood from the coastline of Peru cannot be faulted.
It is varied, flavorful, and plentiful, due, in large part, to the largesse of
the Humboldt Current. This soup is a vivid example of what the very
freshest of seafood can produce in taste.*

8	cups (2 quarts) water
¾	cup rice, well rinsed, soaked in cold water ½ hour, and drained
2	ears of corn, fresh or frozen, cut into 2-inch rounds
2	pounds (6) white or yellow potatoes, peeled and quartered
2	sprigs cilantro
1	pound medium shrimp in the shell, well rinsed
2	cloves garlic, chopped
1	small onion, chopped (¼ cup)
¼	cup chopped ripe tomato
1	teaspoon salt
1	tablespoon corn oil
6	fried eggs

1. Bring the water to a boil in a large pot over moderate heat. Add the rice, corn, potatoes, cilantro, and shrimp.

2. Meanwhile, in a medium skillet stir-fry the garlic, onion, tomato, and salt in the oil for 2 minutes. Add to the soup. Simmer the mixture over low heat for 15 minutes, or until the potatoes are soft.

Serve hot, in bowls, with 1 fried egg per person as garnish on top.
Serves 6

Chupe de Camarones del Rio (Iquitos)

FRESHWATER SHRIMP SOUP

During the rainy season, freshwater shrimp are caught on the Peruvian side of the Amazon River. They are sweeter in flavor than their saltwater cousins and noted for their size and availability at that time of year.

8	cups (2 quarts) water
2	pounds whole freshwater shrimp with head, well rinsed
1	tablespoon corn oil
3	cloves garlic, ground to a paste with 2 tablespoons of water
½	teaspoon turmeric
¼	teaspoon pepper
¼	teaspoon cumin
1	potato, peeled and cut into ¼-inch dice (1 cup)
½	pound thin dried spaghetti, broken in half
3	eggs, beaten
2	cups milk
½	teaspoon salt, or to taste
2	teaspoons dried oregano

1. Bring the water to a boil in a large pot. Add the shrimp, and simmer over low heat for 5 minutes.

2. Meanwhile, heat the oil in a skillet. Add the garlic, turmeric, pepper, and cumin and stir-fry over low heat for 1 minute. Add to the shrimp and broth.

3. Add the potato and spaghetti and simmer for 15 minutes. Stir the beaten eggs into the broth. Add the milk, salt, and oregano and bring to a simmer.

Serve hot, with rice. **Serves 8 to 10**

Chupe de Camarones del Rio (Arequipa)

SPECIAL FRESHWATER SHRIMP SOUP

*The rivers of Peru, including the Amazon, have a surfeit of shrimp,
also known as crayfish and* langousta. *The shrimp are caught during the
rainy season and this soup can be prepared at that time. However, saltwater
shrimp can also be used here, but their flavor is somewhat different,
and is missing the sweetness of the river shrimp.*

1	tablespoon corn oil
1	small onion, diced (⅓ cup)
2	cloves garlic, crushed
1	teaspoon paprika
¼	teaspoon cumin
4	whole allspice
1	teaspoon salt, or to taste
7	cups water
1-1½	pounds whole freshwater shrimp with heads, well rinsed
2	ears of corn, husked and each cut into 4 rounds
½	cup shelled fresh fava beans (optional)
5	small potatoes, peeled and quartered (1 pound)
½	pound *Zapallo* (see Glossary) or butternut squash, peeled and cut into ½ -inch cubes
½	cup rice
2	eggs, beaten
¼	cup evaporated milk
¼	pound mozzarella cheese, cut into ½-inch cubes
1	tablespoon *huacatay* (see Glossary)

1. Heat the oil in a large pan. Add the onion, garlic, paprika, cumin, allspice, and salt and stir-fry over low heat for 2 minutes. Add the water and bring to a boil.

2. Add the shrimp, corn, fava beans, potatoes, and squash and simmer the mixture over low heat for ½ hour. Add the rice. When it is almost soft, often about 10 minutes, add the 2 eggs and cook for 2 minutes.

3. Stir in the milk, cheese, and *huacatay*. Adjust the salt to taste and simmer for 5 minutes.

Serve hot. **Serves 8**

Parihuela Peruana (Japanese)
SEAFOOD SOUP

I watched and listened as the Peruvian-Japanese chef (a woman) went through the motions and measurements of this soup. It does not differ much from the Peruvian version and is not a Japanese invention, but something accommodated to in the new country.

4	cups (1 quart) water
1	½-pound whole red snapper, sea bass, or similar fish, cleaned, with head and tail
1	tablespoon corn oil
1	medium onion, sliced (1 cup)
4	cloves garlic, chopped
2	teaspoons chopped ginger
1	teaspoon dried oregano
4	bay leaves
1	teaspoon salt, or to taste
½	teaspoon pepper
½	cup tomato sauce, homemade or canned
1	tablespoon white wine
¾	cup small shrimp, peeled and deveined
¾	cup sliced squid
6	small hard-shelled clams, steamed briefly and removed from shells
6	mussels, steamed briefly to open and removed from shells
2	crabs, top shell removed, bottom cut into 4 pieces

1. Cut the fish crosswise into 6 pieces. Put the fish pieces plus the head in a large pan, add the water, and bring to a boil. Simmer over low heat for 20 minutes.

2. Meanwhile, heat the oil in a wok or large skillet. Add the onion, garlic, ginger, oregano, bay leaves, salt, and pepper and stir-fry over low heat for 3 minutes. Add the mixture to the fish broth. Stir in the tomato sauce, wine, shrimp, squid, clams, mussels, and crabs and simmer the soup gently for 15 minutes.

Serve hot. **Serves 6 to 8**

Chilcano de Pirana (Iquitos)

PIRANHA BROTH

Piranha have a terrible reputation as a predatory fish that moves in schools, attacking anything in sight. A freshwater fish of the Amazon, they are small in size and benevolent-looking (not like a saint, of course), but not dangerous either, until you see their open mouths at the fishmongers in the public market where their razor-sharp little white teeth tell a different story.

Depending upon the freshwater flavor of the fish you use, this is a clean-tasting, clear broth.

4	piranha, about 1 pound (see Note)
2	cups water
1	clove garlic, ground to a paste
½	teaspoon salt, or to taste
2	scallions (known as Chinese onion), cut into 1-inch pieces
2	sprigs fresh cilantro, chopped

1. Clean the fish, remove the gills, and rinse the fish in cold water.

2. In a wide pan, bring the water to a boil. Add the fish, garlic, and salt and cover. Cook over moderate heat for 8 minutes.

3. Add the scallions and cilantro and cook for 2 minutes. The broth will be clear and full of flavor and the fish tender.

Serve warm, 1 fish per person, with the broth. **Serves 4**

Note: Since piranha are hard to come by, I suggest substituting small lake fish, such as perch or sunfish.

Sopa de Maiz (Cuzco)
FRESH CORN SOUP

The Convento Santa Clara is on Calle Concebidayoc at the edge of the sprawling public market of Cuzco. As I was passing there one day, it occurred to me that the nuns of that cloistered convent would be the guardians of the earliest colonial recipes. I wandered into the main courtyard; not a soul was in sight. A cleaning woman came by and told me to ring a bell near the unmarked entrance to the convent.

I did, and in a moment a voice spoke to me through the revolving wood speaker by which the nuns communicated with outsiders. No one was visible and a woman's voice asked my mission. I introduced myself and told her the reason for my inquiry. The Madre told me to return the next day at the same hour, by which time she would find the oldest recipe in the convent that was still being served in the dining room. I did and here is the recipe, from the Sixteenth Century: a vegetarian soup.

6	fresh ears of corn, husked
3	tablespoons corn oil
1	large onion, chopped (1 cup)
6	cloves garlic, chopped
1	teaspoon finely chopped seeded *aji* amarillo (yellow Peruvian chili, see Glossary), or 1 teaspoon dried yellow *aji* chili powder
12	cups (3 quarts) hot water
2	teaspoons salt, or to taste
1	cup cubed *queso fresco* (see Glossary) or Feta cheese
10	eggs

1. Cut the kernels off the ears of corn and set aside.

2. Heat the oil in a large pan. Add the onion, garlic, and *aji* and stir-fry over low heat until the onion turns golden. Add the water, little by little, until it comes to a boil.

3. Add the corn kernels and salt and mix in the *queso fresco.*

4. Finally, crack 1 egg at a time into the simmering soup. Cover the pan for 5 minutes, then remove it from the heat.

Serve hot, in bowls, with 1 egg per person. **Serves 10**

Sopa a la Criolla (Trujillo)
CREOLE SOUP

The Criolla are the descendants of the original Conquistadores and the indigenous people of Peru that they encountered. They are also the old-time cooks who used clay pots that simmered for long periods of time over wood fires. In earlier times, criolla women spent most of their time preparing food for large families without modern short cuts. Curiously, this soup could almost qualify as fast food: simple ingredients, seasoned in Peruvian fashion, and combined rapidly.

1	tablespoon corn oil
½	pound tender beef steak, cut in 1-inch thin slices
½	teaspoon salt
⅛	teaspoon pepper
1	clove garlic, chopped fine
1	teaspoon dried oregano
1	tablespoon chopped onion
2	tablespoons chopped tomato
5	cups beef broth or water
¼	pound thin dried spaghetti, broken into 3-inch pieces
6	eggs
½	cup milk

1. Heat the oil in a wide, large pan. Add the beef, salt, pepper, garlic, and oregano and stir-fry over moderate heat for 1 minute.

2. Add the onion and tomato and stir-fry for 3 minutes. Add the broth or water and bring to a boil. Add the spaghetti and cook the mixture for 10 minutes.

3. Break the eggs, 1 at a time, carefully into the hot broth. Stir in the milk and cook slowly, for 3 minutes until combined.

Serve hot, in bowl, with 1 egg per person. **Serves 6**

Sopa de Trigo (Cuzco)

BEEF AND VEGETABLE SOUP WITH WHEAT KERNELS

Cuzco, the antique and proud city of the Quechua nation, lies at about 10,000 feet elevation. There is a shortage of oxygen at that height and travelers are warned not to move too fast in the brilliant sun and rarefied atmosphere. A good strong cup of mate de coca *is recommended to ward off the effects of the altitude. Prepared from the green leaves of the coca plant (which produces the vicious cocaine), the tea is not addictive and is also a digestive, among its other wondrous characteristics.*

At dusk in Cuzco, the temperature plummets and at night it is downright cold. So one begins to consider a large bowl of the richly flavored, substantial sopa de trigo that is prepared with whole wheat kernels, beef, several vegetables, and, of course, the ubiquitous potato, which Peruvian cooking never seems to be without. The soup is guaranteed to ward off the penetrating chill that settles over the city.

16   **cups (4 quarts) water**

1 ½ **pounds beef chuck, with or without bones, cut into 1-inch cubes**

1   **cup whole wheat kernels, soaked in water overnight and drained**

4   **cloves garlic, chopped fine**

1   **stalk celery, chopped**

1   **leek, white part only, rinsed well and chopped**

1   **pound *Zapallo* (see Glossary) or butternut squash, peeled and cut into 1-inch cubes (see Note)**

2   **large carrots, cut in 1½-inch cubes (1½ cups)**

1   **large potato (½ pound), peeled and cut into 1-inch cubes**

1   **cup fresh or frozen peas**

2   **teaspoons salt, or to taste**

8   **whole peppercorns**

½   **pound fresh spinach leaves**

1   **teaspoon dried oregano**

1   **sprig fresh mint, chopped**

1   **sprig cilantro, chopped**

1   **sprig flat-leaf parsley, chopped**

1. Put the water, beef, wheat kernels, and garlic into a large pot and bring to a boil. Simmer over low heat until the meat and wheat kernels are tender, about 40 minutes.

2. Add the celery, leek, squash, carrots, potato, and green peas and simmer, covered, until the vegetables are almost soft, about 15 minutes. Stir in the salt, peppercorns, and spinach.

3. Sprinkle the oregano, mint, cilantro, and parley over the top and simmer 5 minutes. Adjust the salt to taste.

Serve hot. **Serves 8 to 10**

Note: All over Peru one sees the giant *zapallo*, an enormous winter squash with a hard outer shell and brilliant orange pulp. It is sold by the kilo and is a popular vegetable in soups and purées. In Vermont, where I was raised, we put the hard-shelled Hubbard squash to good use over the lengthy winters.

Almuerzo de Quinoa (Cuzco)
QUINOA SOUP FOR LUNCH

Quinoa was known to the Incas and is now known by their descendants, especially in the upper altitudes of Peru. This hearty soup for lunch contains all the traditional and typical ingredients of the countryside.

3	cups quinoa, rinsed, soaked in cold water for 1 hour and drained
9	cups water for cooking the quinoa
2	tablespoons corn oil
3	cloves garlic, crushed
2	medium onions, chopped (1 cup)
¼	teaspoon cumin
¼	teaspoon pepper
1	teaspoon dried yellow *aji* chili powder (see Glossary)
10	cups (2½ quarts) water for the soup

2	teaspoons salt, or to taste
3	pounds shoulder lamb chops with bone, trimmed and cut into 12 pieces
3	carrots, cut in little-finger-sized pieces
1	pound potato, peeled and cut into 12 equal pieces
½	cup shelled fresh fava beans (optional)
1	tablespoon chopped fresh cilantro
2	teaspoons dried oregano

1. Simmer the quinoa in the 9 cups of water, stirring frequently, for about 20 minutes. (Quinoa expands and becomes translucent when cooked.) Drain and set aside.

2. Heat the oil in a pan. Add the garlic, onions, cumin, pepper, and chili powder and stir-fry over low heat for 2 minutes. Add the 10 cups of water and salt and bring to a boil. Add the lamb pieces.

3. Add the carrots and potato and simmer over low heat for 15 minutes. Add the fava beans (if used) and quinoa and cook for 10 minutes. Adjust the salt if necessary.

Garnish with the cilantro and oregano.

Serve hot. **Serves 10 to 12**

Sopa de Carnero y Quinoa (Cuzco)

LAMB AND QUINOA SOUP

The Incas knew about the health-promoting properties of quinoa and ate it in a variety of ways. What they did not know was that quinoa, which resembles a small version of sesame seeds, contained 12 to 22 percent protein, and its sister seed, "kanigua" contained 15 to 30 percent protein. Since the Incas did not have the cow, pig, sheep, or goat, all of which were introduced by the Spanish after the Conquest, quinoa actually acted as the vegetable protein.

1	tablespoon corn oil
1	medium onion, chopped
2	cloves garlic, crushed
½	teaspoon paprika
¼	teaspoon cumin
8	cups (2 quarts) water
2	pounds lamb, with or without bone, cut into 2-inch pieces
1	cup quinoa, rinsed, soaked in cold water for 1 hour and drained
1	teaspoon salt, or to taste
1	pound potatoes, peeled and cubed
1	carrot, cut into ¼-inch dice (1 cup)
½	cup fresh or frozen green peas

1. Heat the oil in a pan. Add the onion, garlic, paprika, and cumin and stir-fry over low heat for 2 minutes. Add the water, bring to a boil, and add the lamb. Cook, covered, for 15 minutes.

2. Add the quinoa and simmer for 15 minutes. (It will swell.) Add the salt, potatoes, carrot, and green peas, cover, and cook for 15 minutes, or until the meat and vegetables are soft. Adjust the salt to taste. (The quinoa will become translucent and will have a mild nut-like taste.)

Serve hot. **Serves 8**

Caldo de Carnero (Trujillo)

LAMB AND VEGETABLE SOUP

Hearty lamb flavor, vegetables, and pasta make this an ideal soup for cold weather.

10	cups (2½ quarts) water
1	teaspoon salt
2	pounds lamb ribs with bone, trimmed of fat
½	pound *Zapallo* (see Glossary) or butternut squash, cut into 1-inch cubes
1	carrot, cut into finger-sized lengths
1	small leek, halved and well rinsed
1	stalk celery, halved
1	ear of corn, cut into 2-inch rounds
1	medium potato, peeled and cut into 1-inch cubes (1 cup)
1	small white turnip, peeled and sliced (½ cup)
½	pound dried spaghetti (#8)
½	teaspoon dried oregano
1	teaspoon chopped fresh cilantro

1. Bring the water and salt to a boil in a large pot. Add the lamb, and simmer, covered, over low heat for ½ hour.

2. Add the squash, carrot, leek, celery, corn, potato, turnip, and spaghetti and simmer for 20 minutes. Remove and discard the leek and celery. Add the oregano and cilantro and adjust the salt to taste.

Serve hot. **Serves 8**

Sopa Chambar (Trujillo)

WHOLE KERNEL WHEAT SOUP

Is this a stew or a thick soup of wheat kernels, potatoes, chick peas, and white beans? In fact, it is an old-time Quechua recipe, which is served during the cold weather, that sometimes contains a pig's ear (optional) and very little meat. Meat is money, and a little bit goes a long way, as it does here.

2	cups whole wheat kernels
¼	cup dried fava beans
¼	cup dried white beans
¼	cup dried garbanzo beans (chick peas)
I	pig's ear (optional)
6	cups (1½ quarts) water
I	pound smoked ham, cut into little-finger-sized pieces and rinsed in hot water
I	tablespoon corn oil
2	cloves garlic, chopped fine
I	tablespoon chopped onion
½	teaspoon salt, or to taste
¼	teaspoon paprika
½	teaspoon dried oregano

1. Cover the wheat kernels with water and soak overnight. Drain and discard loose peelings. In separate bowls, soak the fava beans, white beans, and garbanzo beans overnight. Drain and remove the skins, which should peel off easily.

2. In a large pot cook the pig's ear (if used), wheat kernels, and all the beans in the water, covered, over low heat, for 1 hour. Add the ham and simmer ½ hour.

3. Meanwhile, heat the oil in a skillet. Add the garlic, onion, salt, and paprika and cook until the mixture is browned, about 2 minutes. Stir in the oregano.

4. Add the onion mixture to the soup. Add more water if the soup is too thick and stir frequently to prevent burning.

Serve hot. **Serves 8 to 10**

Caldo de Gallina Regional (Iquitos)
REGIONAL SOUP OF THE AMAZON

A seven- to eight-pound hen is preferred by the home cooks in the public market who make chicken soup for their customers. The very simple eating booths (they could never be considered restaurants) provide clean, simple regional food at modest prices. The flavor of a hen is more intense than that of a three-pound chicken and the firmer meat of the hen is desired in a soup. To each, his own.

10	cups water
3	pounds hen parts, cut into 10 portions
2	teaspoons salt, or to taste
2	cloves garlic, chopped
I	pound spaghetti (#8), broken in half
6	sprigs fresh cilantro, chopped
2	pounds yuca (see Glossary), peeled, cut into 3-inch fingers, and cooked

1. Bring the water to a boil in a large pot. Add the hen pieces, salt, and garlic, cover the pot and cook over low heat for 45 minutes, or until the meat is tender.

2. Add the spaghetti and coriander and simmer for 15 minutes (or less, if you prefer the pasta *al dente*).

Serve the chicken, spaghetti, and broth hot. If desired, add the cooked yuca to the soup. **Serves 10**

Caldo de Gallina Estilo Cuzco (Cuzco)

HEN SOUP CUZCO STYLE

The central market in Cuzco is a sight to behold, especially the food kiosks that offer traditional dishes to the Peruvians and any foreigners with an ounce of adventure. The large pots of simmering hen soup—the Peruvians prefer large, meaty hens to the common chicken—is full of flavor and popular. A large bowl costs less than $2.00.

12	cups (3 quarts) water
4	pounds hen parts (thighs, legs, or breasts), cut into 10 serving pieces
2	stalks celery hearts, chopped
2	small carrots, cut into little finger-sized pieces
1	small onion, chopped (½ cup)
2	scallions, chopped
3	cloves garlic, crushed
1	1-inch piece fresh ginger, crushed
2	teaspoons salt, or to taste
2	whole allspice
1½ pounds dried pasta, shells or another small shape	

1. Bring the water to a boil in a large pot. Add the hen pieces and simmer over low heat, skimming the foam that rises to the surface, for ½ hour, or until the meat is tender.

2. Add the celery, carrots, onion, scallions, garlic, ginger, salt, and allspice and simmer for 10 minutes. Add the pasta and cook until it is *al dente* (or softer if desired), about 15 minutes.

Serve hot. **Serves 8 to 10**

Inchicapi de Gallina (Iquitos)

HEN SOUP WITH GROUND PEANUTS AND CORNMEAL

This is jungle food, and it is not so much a soup as it is a gruel since the cornmeal and ground peanuts serve as thickeners. The all-pervasive flavor, along with that of the hen, is ultimately enticing. Note: Yuca and cassava are the same root vegetable. For more information on it, see the Glossary.

10	cups (2½ quarts) water
3	pounds hen parts, both light and dark meat, cut into 10 serving pieces
2	teaspoons salt, or to taste
¼	cup dry roasted peanuts, ground but not too fine
¼	cup cornmeal
2	cloves garlic, ground to a paste with 2 tablespoons water
6	sprigs fresh cilantro, chopped
2	pounds yuca root, peeled and cut into thick finger-sized pieces

1. Bring the water to a boil in a large pot. Add the hen pieces and salt and cook over low heat, skimming off the foam that rises to the surface, for 45 minutes, or until the meat is tender.

2. Add the ground peanuts, cornmeal, garlic paste, and cilantro and combine very well. Cook over low heat for ½ hour, stirring frequently. (If the liquid evaporates too quickly, add more water to make a smooth soup/gruel.)

3. Cook the yuca separately in boiling water to cover until soft, about 20 minutes. Drain and serve the yuca separately.

Serve warm. **Serves 10**

Caldo de 7 Carnes (Arequipa)

SOUP OF 7 MEATS

*This particular version of this flavorful soup has only five different meats,
but one could add llama, kid, turkey, or duck, all Peruvian favorites.
Like so many of the foods of Arequipa, the soup is an inventive
combination, made with ingredients of the countryside.*

16   cups (4 quarts) water

1   pound lamb, with or without bone, cut into 6 pieces

1   pound boneless beef, cut into 6 pieces

1   pound boneless chicken breast, cut into 6 pieces

2   lamb tongues, cooked, skinned, and
     halved lengthwise

¼   pound *cecina* (smoked dried beef, available in
     Latin markets), cut into 6 pieces

¼   cup cooked chick peas

4   cloves garlic, crushed

1   stalk celery, sliced thin

1   leek, white part only, sliced and well rinsed

1   teaspoon dried oregano

½   pound potato, peeled and cut into 6 pieces

6   small white *chuno* (freeze-dried potatoes,
     see Glossary; optional)

½   pound yuca, peeled and cut into
     6 thumb-sized pieces

1   teaspoon salt, or to taste

6   whole peppercorns

2   cups cooked rice

2   tablespoons chopped parsley, for garnish

1. Bring the water to a boil in a large pot over high heat. Reduce the
heat to moderate and add the lamb, beef, chicken, tongue, *cecina*, chick
peas, garlic, celery, leek, and oregano. Cover and cook for 25 minutes.

2. Add the potato, *chuno* (if used), yuca, salt, and peppercorns and simmer over low heat for 30 minutes, or until all the meats are tender.

To serve, divide the meats and vegetables evenly among soup bowls, add 2 tablespoons cooked rice to each bowl, and garnish with parsley.

Serve hot. **Serves 6 to 8**

Sopa Especial Kun Fu (Peruvian/Japanese)
SPECIAL SOUP WITH MEAT, SEAFOOD, AND VEGETABLES

"Kun Fu" is a Chinese term that has been borrowed by the Japanese who have given it their own particular twist. This soup contains many ingredients and has both substance and flavor.

1	pound dried spaghetti (#8 size)
1	teaspoon salt
⅓	cup corn oil
1	tablespoon garlic, chopped fine
9	cups Fish Broth (page 35)
8	clams hard-shelled
¾	cup chopped (not ground) beef
¾	cup chopped (not ground) chicken breast
6	eggs
¾	cup medium shrimp, peeled and deveined
¾	cup sliced squid rings
¾	cup whole small scallops
1	cup thinly sliced sweet red pepper
1	cup thinly sliced celery heart
1	cup thinly sliced onion
1	cup thinly sliced Napa cabbage

1. Cook the spaghetti with the salt in a large pot of boiling water for 15 minutes. Drain, rinse under cold water, and drain again. Set aside.

2. Heat the oil in a large skillet. Add the garlic and stir-fry for a few seconds. Add the fish broth and bring to a boil. Add the clams, beef, and chicken, and simmer for 5 minutes.

3. Add the eggs, 1 at a time, and simmer 5 minutes.

4. Add all the seafood and the spaghetti and simmer for 1 minute.

5. Add all the vegetables and simmer for 1 minute only so that they remain crisp.

Serve hot, with a little of everything in each bowl. **Serves 6 to 8**

CIVDAD
LAVILLADEPISQVI

SEAFOOD OF ALL KINDS

When one considers the seafood dishes of Peru, one thinks immediately, with enthusiasm, of *ceviche*—the raw fish tidbits cooked (not really) in lime juice. There are many combinations of *ceviche*, a mixture of fish, scallops, squid, octopus with onion, chili, cilantro, and whatever else the personal preference of the cook dictates. But there are many more enticing Peruvian seafood dishes in the pages that follow.

For the inexhaustible source of Peru's seafood, one should be aware of the Humboldt Current, a cold, broad, shallow current of water that flows along the western coast of Peru north of the Equator. This current carries a wealth of marine organisms that provide food for vast numbers of fish that are caught for Peruvian domestic and foreign markets. Seafood is king, and so are the myriad numbers of recipes from the diverse regions of Peru—the coast, the Andes, and the tropical Amazon.

The indigenous populations of creole, Chinese, Negro, Japanese, Italian, and Quechua Incas in the highland altiplano all contribute their ethnic fish preparations. Peruvians can be thankful for the quantity, quality, and variety of their natural bounty from the sea.

Ceviche de Pescado (Trujillo)

FISH SALAD COOKED IN LIME JUICE

*The English title of this recipe is not an altogether accurate description of
ceviche since it is the lime (or lemon juice) that "cooks" the fish.*

*Peruvians are justifiably proud of their internationally famous method
of serving fish tidbits. A mixed assortment can include squid, octopus,
scallops, clams, langostas, as well as pata de mula, a shellfish similar to
scallops. Then there are the black scallops of Peru, a rarity. All can be
used in a classic ceviche, insuring a variety of textures and flavors.*

2	pounds white-fleshed skinless fish fillets such as flounder, sole, or *corvina* (cod)
I	cup fresh lime juice (about 12 limes)
½	teaspoon salt
I	small clove garlic, chopped very fine
I	or 2 fresh *aji amarillo* (yellow Peruvian chili, see Glossary), seeded and chopped fine, or substitute the canned *aji*
I	teaspoon chopped parsley
I	teaspoon chopped cilantro
I	medium onion, chopped fine (½ cup)
3	or 4 lettuce leaves
4	ears of corn, cooked and cut into 2-inch pieces
I	pound sweet potatoes, cooked in the skin, peeled, and sliced into ½-inch-thick rounds
I	pound yuca (see Glossary), peeled, cut in little-finger-sized slices and cooked
	A few strands of *yuyo* (free seaweed, optional, see Glossary)

1. Cut the fish into strips 1½ inches long and ¼ inch wide. Soak the
strips in lightly salted water for 1 hour to tenderize. Drain well.

2. Put the fish in a bowl and fold in the lime juice carefully. Add the
salt, garlic, and *aji* and refrigerate for 15 to 20 minutes.

3. Just before serving, mix in the parsley, cilantro, and onion.

4. To serve, line a bowl or large platter with the lettuce. Place the *ceviche* in the center. Surround it with 3 separate mounds: corn pieces at the top of the platter, sweet potato slices on one end, yuca on the other. Garnish with the seaweed, if using. **Serves 6**

Ceviche Simple Estilo (Cuzco)
CEVICHE CUZCO STYLE

I used to go to the Mercado Central (San Pedro) in Cuzco every day to buy fruit and look for new prepared foods. Of course, it included having my ceviche *fix about 11 AM, which was prepared by the kiosk vendor who referred to it as "simple."*

It was served on a plate on a large lettuce leaf, with a garnish of thick slices of sweet potato and a handful of roasted giant white corn known as choclo.

2	**pounds skinless fillet of flounder, sea bass, or similar fish, cut into ¼-inch cubes**
½	**cup fresh lime juice**
I	**teaspoon salt, or more to taste**
⅛	**teaspoon pepper**
⅓	**cup sliced celery heart**
5	**cloves garlic, sliced thin**
I	**slice fresh ginger, peeled and diced**
I	**fresh *aji amarillo* (yellow Peruvian chili, see Glossary), seeded and sliced or the canned *aji* substitute**
I	**pound small red onions, peeled and sliced thin**
8	**lettuce leaves**
I	**pound sweet potato, cooked in the skin until soft, peeled, and sliced thick**
	Choclo (see Note), for serving
I	**tablespoon chopped fresh cilantro, for garnish**

1. Mix the fish cubes with lime juice, salt, and pepper and set aside for ½ hour. Stir now and then.

2. In a food processor, process the celery, garlic, ginger, and *aji* to a moderately thick consistency. Stir into the fish mixture.

3. At the moment of serving, add the onions, and mix well.

Serve on a lettuce leaf with a slice of sweet potato on the side with a handful of roast corn in a side dish. Garnish with cilantro. **Serves 8 or more**

Note: Large corn kernels that are roasted, like peanuts, and served as a snack with drinks or as a garnish with *ceviche*. *Choclo* is often found in ethnic food stores.

Sazimi Peruana (Ceviche Japones)
PERUVIAN/JAPANESE CEVICHE

The Japanese community, primarily in Lima, is small, tightly knit, and energetic. Their cuisine has been modified only to coordinate with existing ingredients found in Peru. Their influence on the general style of Peruvian cooking is nonexistent, unlike the influence of the Chinese whose cooking techniques and flavors have been accepted throughout the country.

Nevertheless, the President of Peru, Fujimori, is Japanese, and this highly prestigious appointment has instilled the community with an additional sense of pride and loyalty. But the cooking is oriental in appearance and taste. It is also one of the cross-cultural cuisines found in Peru.

2 ½ pounds fillets of flounder, cod, or similar white fish
½   pound daikon (white radish), peeled
2   cucumbers, peeled and trimmed

1. Cut the fish fillets into slices 1 ½-inch long by ¼-inch wide. Set aside.

2. Grate the daikon on the fine side of a square box grater.

3. Cut the cucumber in half lengthwise. Scoop out and discard the seeds and slice each half into thin half moons.

Like all Japanese cooking, sashimi is meticulously sliced and arranged on a serving platter as follows: Arrange the fish in the center of an oblong platter. Place the cucumber along the top edge of the platter, the grated daikon along the bottom edge. Diners will select fish, cucumber, or daikon, dip it into the sashimi sauce (recipe follows), and eat with rice.

THE SAUCE

½	cup soy sauce
½	teaspoon finely grated ginger
I	teaspoon fresh lime juice
¼	teaspoon wasabi paste

Mix all the sauce ingredients together and set aside for 15 minutes before serving to allow the flavors to integrate. Serve at room temperature.

Chilcano de Pescado (Santa Rosa, near Chiclayo)
FISH CHOWDER AT THE PORT

On the day that I visited the fishing port of Santa Rosa there were not many boats out. The waves were high, the wind was whistling down the main street that is lined with bars cum eating houses, and the sky was gray. The seediness of the town was never more apparent. But the food was excellent!

Corvina (cod) is a much-esteemed fish along the Peruvian coast and is recommended if you can find it. Otherwise, sea bass, red snapper, tile fish, or another similar fish will work very well here. In Santa Rosa the fish go from the sea to the kitchen to the table in rapid order.

4	cups (1 quart) water (see Note)
1	teaspoon salt, or to taste
1	tablespoon corn oil
2	teaspoons finely chopped, seeded fresh *aji amarillo* (yellow Peruvian chili, see Glossary), or 1 teaspoon dried yellow *aji* chili powder
6	sprigs fresh cilantro, chopped
	A 3-pound *corvina* (cod), the whole fish cleaned and cut crosswise into 3-inch pieces, including the head but not the tail (see Note)

1. Bring water to a boil in a large pan. Add the salt, oil, *aji*, and cilantro and simmer over moderate heat for 5 minutes. Add the fish pieces, cover the pan, and cook for 15 to 20 minutes.

Serve each diner at least 1 slice of fish, with the broth. There is always someone who loves the desirable fish head.

Serve hot. **Serves 5**

Note: Fish head concentrate may be used instead of water. Here is how it is done in Chiclayo: Cook 5 five heads, gills removed, in 5 cups water with 1 teaspoon salt, 6 sprigs fresh cilantro, and 2 sliced scallions in a pan, covered, over moderate heat for 20 minutes. Strain and use instead of the quart of water in the chowder.

Parihuela (Trujillo)

FISHERMAN'S SOUP/STEW

I was told by my teacher that parihuela *is a criolla word of the Trujillo fishermen, the inventors of this dish. Like so many of the titles relating to recipes in Peru, a translation is hard to find and probably lost in the past.*

12 cups (3 quarts) water

    A 1-pound large fish head, well rinsed and gills removed

1   pound fresh snails in the shell

1   pound small hard-shelled clams

1   pound mussels, scrubbed

1   pound scallops, in the shell if possible

1   pound squid, cleaned and sliced into rounds

1   fish roe, such as tuna or other popular fish (available in season)

1   cup dry white wine

1   tablespoon cornstarch, dissolved in ¼ cup cold water

1   tablespoon corn oil

2   cloves garlic, chopped fine

1   medium onion, chopped (½ cup)

2   teaspoons paprika

1   tablespoon finely chopped seeded fresh *aji amarillo* (yellow Peruvian chili, see Glossary), or 2 teaspoons dried yellow *aji* chili powder

¼   cup chopped tomato

2   stalks celery, remove strings and sliced

1   small leek, white and green parts, rinsed well and sliced

1   teaspoon salt

¼   teaspoon pepper

½   pound medium shrimp, peeled and deveined

½   pound skinless *corvina* (cod) or flounder fillet, cut into little-finger-sized pieces

2   whole crabs, top shell on each removed and set aside

1. Bring the water to a boil in a large pot. Add the fish head and cook over moderate heat for 10 minutes. Then add the snails, clams, mussels, scallops, squid, and fish roe and cook for 5 minutes. Strain into another pot. Let the shellfish cool. Stir wine into the broth. Stir in the cornstarch mixture. Set the broth aside.

2. Remove all the shellfish from their shells. Discard shells.

3. Heat the oil in a skillet. Add the garlic, onion, paprika, *aji*, tomato, celery, and leek and stir-fry over moderate heat for 3 minutes. Add the mixture to the broth. Add salt and pepper to taste, if needed.

4. Bring the broth to a boil over moderate heat. Add all the shellfish to the broth. Add the strips of *corvina* or flounder, the crabs with the top shells, and the shrimp, simmer everything for 5 minutes, until cooked through.

Serve hot. **Serves 10**

The Shipibo Indians (Amazon)

I met two Amazonian Shipibo Indians in front of my hotel in Iquitos with an armload of handwoven and handpainted cloth from Pnuyan, their village of 1,500 inhabitants. It took them four days in a river boat to come to the city and four days to return to the village in the jungle with some money (not much) and market goods they needed.

They wore the colorful costume of the village, a blouse made of machine-woven fabric, a skirt and sash, and it seemed as if they had dressed in a hurry. They were striking women with long, straight, jet-black hair. We spoke in Spanish. The older woman, who had seven children, told me in her soft, courteous voice that their diet consisted mainly of various kinds of fish from the Amazon, plus wild animals such as peccary, monkeys, and wild fowl. The food was cooked over wood fires in clay pots that had been made by the family during the dry season.

Many jungle fruit were eaten by them during the season, such as mango, *sapote, caimito,* guava, and orange. Other sweets included honey, papaya, and sweet potatoes.

The Shipibo planted white and natural brown cotton for their weavings. They raised chickens, ducks, and turkeys for sale or their own use.

Here is a recipe of their most common food—river fish.

Caldo de Pescado

FISH SOUP

The soup is cooked in a large clay pot for as long as needed to soften the fish and plantains.

Family members help themselves whenever they want to and since there is no shortage of fish they can replenish the soup pot or prepare it again later in the day.

4	quarts water
6	or more ripe or green plantains, quartered
10	assorted river fish, whatever was caught for the meal
	Salt to taste

Bring the water to a boil over an outdoor wood fire. Add the fish, if large, cut into pieces, and if small, whole. Add the plantains. Cook for as long as necessary.

Pescado al Horno (Chincha)

SIMPLE BAKED FISH

Any fish of a reasonable size from the Humboldt Current can be baked. Since fish is the principle food along the coast of Peru there is a continuous source of economical eating. This simple preparation has Peruvian trademarks—yuca, French fries, and rice.

3	1¼ pound whole red snapper or similar fish, cleaned
4	cloves garlic, ground to a paste with 2 tablespoons water
¼	teaspoon salt, or to taste
⅛	teaspoon pepper
1	tablespoon butter, softened
	Juice of 3 lemons

1. Score the fish on both sides with 2 parallel cuts lengthwise. Then make 3 cuts crosswise, resulting in a pattern of squares.

2. In a bowl, combine the garlic paste, salt, pepper, butter, and lemon juice. Rub the marinade into the scored pattern on the fish. (If you feel that you would like more marinade, then prepare another batch.)

3. Place the fish in a baking pan or Pyrex dish and bake in a preheated 350 degree oven for 15 to 20 minutes, or until done.

Serve warm, with boiled yuca, boiled potatoes or French fries, and white rice—any or all of the three. **Serves 6**

Pescado a lo Macho (Callao)

FISH FOR MEN

Macho is really translated as masculine, male or strong, among other definitions. It has great sexual connotation. But how to equate this with a fish!

2	pounds fillets of cod, flounder, or similar fish, cut into 8 pieces
1	teaspoon salt
4	cloves garlic, ground to a paste with 2 tablespoons water
½	cup flour
¼	cup corn oil
1	medium onion, chopped (½ cup)
1	teaspoon ginger, ground to a paste with 1 tablespoon water
2	teaspoons paprika
1	pound squid, cut into rounds
½	pound cooked octopus, sliced thin (see Note, page 103)
¾	cup water

1¼	pounds medium shrimp, peeled and deveined
¼	cup dry white wine
¼	cup coconut milk, preferably Chaokoh brand from Thailand
1	tablespoon cornstarch, dissolved in 3 tablespoons water
2	tablespoons chopped fresh cilantro
	Lemon wedges, for serving

1. Mix the fish pieces with the salt and half of the garlic paste. Dredge the pieces in the flour.

2. Heat the oil in a skillet and fry the fish over low heat for about 3 minutes. Set aside on paper towels to drain.

3. In the skillet, fry the onion, ginger paste, and remaining garlic paste over low heat for 2 minutes. Add the paprika, squid, and octopus and stir to coat. Now add the water and bring to a boil. Add the shrimp, wine, and coconut milk, stirring well to create a sauce. Simmer for 3 minutes, then stir in just enough of the cornstarch mixture to thicken the sauce lightly.

To serve, arrange the fried fish in the center of a large serving platter and top with the seafood sauce. Garnish with the fresh cilantro and lemon wedges. Or, arrange individual servings in the same manner. Serve white rice separately. **Serves 8**

Milanesa de Pescado (Lima)

FISH FILLETS, ITALIAN STYLE

*This tender fried fish was served to me in a private home
in Lima. My hostess told me that it was prepared this way, and probably
introduced as a recipe by her Italian grandmother. At another time and
in another city, I was informed by the cook in a typical Peruvian restaurant
serving traditional foods that they did not know the origin of the dish
but it had always been cooked this way. It does take very many years for a
cross-cultural dish to become the property of the host country.*

3	eggs, beaten
1	teaspoon salt, or to taste
⅛	teaspoon ground pepper
1	clove garlic, chopped very fine
2	tablespoons fine-chopped flat-leaf parsley
2	pounds (4 pieces) fillets of flounder, sole, or similar fish
¼	cup flour
¼	cup corn oil

1. Beat the eggs, salt, pepper, garlic, and parsley together in a wide bowl.

2. Dip each piece of fish in the flour, then into the egg mixture. Let stand in the egg mixture 10 minutes. Remove and reserve egg mixture.

3. Heat the oil over low heat in a skillet large enough to hold the fish. Fry the fillets until light brown on both sides, about 3 minutes. Pour any excess egg mixture over the fish as it fries. Drain briefly on paper towels.

Serve warm, with rice or French fries and several salads. **Serves 4**

Pescado con Salsa Tamarindo (Chinese)

FISH FILLETS IN TAMARIND SAUCE

Although the tamarind sauce called for here does not contain tamarind pulp, so often used in Southeast Asian cooking, its sweet/sour combination of flavors is ideal with fish, of which there are many varieties in the waters of Peru.

	A ½-inch piece of ginger, peeled and sliced
2	**cloves garlic**
½	**teaspoon salt**
½	**teaspoon soy sauce**
2	**tablespoons water**
I	**pound fillets of flounder, sea bass, red snapper, or similar fish, cut into 2 ½-inch pieces**
½	**cup flour**
½	**cup corn oil**
2	**cups heated Tamarind Sauce with Pineapple (page 212)**

1. In a food processor, grind the ginger, garlic, salt, and soy sauce to a paste with the water. Rub the fish all over with the mixture and let stand for 15 minutes. Dredge the fish pieces in the flour.

2. Heat the oil in a skillet and fry the fish over low heat for about 3 minutes, turning the pieces, until browned; do not overcook. Transfer to paper towels to drain.

Serve the fish with tamarind sauce poured over it. **Serves 6**

Pescado Sudado (Callao)

STEAMED FISH FILLETS

Callao is the most important port for the entry and exit of goods to and from Peru. It is the port for Lima. Callao has an established indigenous style of cooking. This is an example.

3	tablespoons corn oil
1	large onion, sliced (1 cup)
2	cloves garlic, chopped fine
2	medium tomatoes, sliced (1 cup)
¼	teaspoon paprika
1	teaspoon salt, or to taste
1½	pounds fillets of flounder, *corvina* (cod), or other white-fleshed fish
½	cup dry white wine
10	sprigs parsley, leaves only, chopped
	Lemon slices, for serving

1. Heat the oil in a large skillet over low heat. Add the onion, garlic, tomatoes, paprika and salt and stir-fry for 2 minutes. Cover the mixture completely with the fish fillets.

2. Add the wine, cover the skillet, and cook for 5 minutes over low heat, which is just enough time to steam the fish. Garnish with the parsley.

Serve with lemon slices, accompanied by sliced boiled potatoes, sliced boiled yuca, or hot white rice. **Serves 6**

Causa Chiclayana (Chiclayo)

FISH FRY WITH VEGETABLES

A causa *is a light lunch or snack that is typically served at weddings or other celebrations. It is a popular dish, assembled in a formulaic ritual known to housewives, as so many popular foods are in Peru. A variety of ingredients must be collected and either boiled, fried, sliced, and blanched before being assembled in a grandiose arrangement with garnishes. A fine party dish and worth all the effort.*

THE ONIONS

½   teaspoon salt
I   tablespoon white vinegar
I   pound onions (2), sliced but not too thin

Bring a pan of water to a boil with the salt and vinegar. Add the onions and blanch quickly, for ½ minute. Drain immediately.

Set aside

THE POTATOES

2   pounds potatoes (4 or 5)
½   teaspoon salt
¼   teaspoon pepper
I   teaspoon fresh lime juice
I   teaspoon corn oil

Cook the potatoes in water to cover the skin until soft. Peel and while still warm mash with the salt, pepper, lime juice, and oil. Set aside.

THE FISH

¼   cup corn oil
2   pounds fillets of flounder or similar fish,
     cut into 8 pieces

Heat the oil in a skillet over moderate heat, add the fish pieces, and fry for 2 minutes on each side. Drain on paper towels; set aside.

THE ASSEMBLY

8   to 10 lettuce leaves

Mashed potatoes (see above)

Fried fish pieces (see above)

2   pounds yuca, peeled, cut into thumb-sized pieces, and cooked

4   ears of corn, cooked and cut into 20 rounds

1   pound sweet potatoes, peeled, cut into thumb-sized pieces, and cooked

2   ripe plantains, with yellow/black skin, cooked in the skin, peeled and sliced on the diagonal

4   hard-boiled eggs, peeled and quartered

16 black olives

THE GARNISH

1   tablespoon corn oil

The blanched onions (see above)

1/4 teaspoon salt

1   teaspoon paprika

2   fresh *aji amarillo* (yellow Peruvian chili, see Glossary), seeded and sliced thin

1. Line a large serving platter with the lettuce leaves. Press the mashed potatoes about ½ inch thick in the center of the platter. Cover the potatoes with the fried fish pieces.

2. Around the perimeter of the platter alternate yuca slices, corn, sweet potato rounds, plantain slices, egg quarters, and olives.

3. Heat the oil in a skillet. Add the onions, salt, paprika, and aji and stir-fry over moderate heat for 2 minutes.

4. Cover the fried fish in the platter with this onion mixture. Garnish with fresh coriander leaves.

Serve at room temperature. **Serves 8**

Filet de Pescado con Salsa de Palta (Lima)

FRIED FISH WITH AVOCADO PURÉE

An unconventional combination. Palta is the longish football-shaped avocado with green skin. Its flavor does not differ from the oval-shaped avocados we are accustomed to seeing here.

1½	**pounds fillets of flounder or similar white-fleshed fish**
¼	**cup fresh lemon juice**
1	**teaspoon salt**
1	**large ripe avocado**
2	**tablespoons olive oil**
1	**teaspoon salt**
⅛	**teaspoon white pepper**
1	**small red onion, chopped fine (⅓ cup)**
1	**tablespoon chopped parsley**
1	**large potato, peeled, boiled, and sliced**

1. Season the fillets with 2 tablespoons of the lemon juice, and ½ teaspoon of the salt and let stand 5 minutes.

2. In a large skillet, heat the oil until hot. Add the fillets and fry them lightly until just cooked through. Let cool, then chill.

3. Peel and pit the avocado. In a bowl mash the avocado, add the remaining 2 tablespoons lemon juice, the olive oil, ½ teaspoon salt, onion, and parsley, and combine well.

4. Line a serving platter with the sliced potato. Place the fish fillets in the center and pour the avocado purée over all.

Serve cold, as an appetizer. **Serves 6**

Pescado Dorado al Ajo (Iquitos)

GARLICKED FRIED FISH

A local recipe that emphasizes garlic, known for its health-promoting properties.

THE FISH

¼   cup fresh lime juice

4   cloves garlic, ground to a paste with 2 tablespoons water

½   teaspoon salt

¼   teaspoon pepper

2   pounds fish fillets (6)

¼   cup corn oil

1. Mix the lime juice, garlic paste, salt, and pepper together briskly. Bathe the fish in the mixture for 3 minutes. Remove the fish and discard the marinade.

2. Heat the oil in a skillet. Add the fish and fry it over moderate heat on both sides for about 3 minutes, until crisp but not overdone. Set aside while making the sauce.

THE SAUCE

2   tablespoons butter

2   cloves garlic, ground to a paste with 2 tablespoons water

¾   cup milk

½   teaspoon salt, or to taste

¼   cup flour mixed with ½ cup water to form a paste

1. Heat the butter in a skillet. Add the garlic paste and fry it over low heat for 2 minutes. Add the milk and salt and stir continuously for 1 minute. Then add just enough of the flour paste to lightly thicken the sauce, stirring for another 2 minutes.

Serve one warm fish fillet per person on a dinner plate and garnish with 2 tablespoons of the white sauce. **Serves 6**

Sudado de Pescado (Callao)

FISH IN ONION AND TOMATO SAUCE

A well-seasoned sauce with red wine vinegar and beer covers flounder fillets or similar fish. Not food of the Incas, but of the modern-day Peruvian gourmet.

Medium shrimp, peeled and deveined, may be used instead of the fish. Or, the rare black scallops, 6 per person, shelled with their liquid. Black scallops are found in Peruvian waters and are sold in some fish markets in Queens, New York.

2	tablespoons corn oil
4	cloves garlic, sliced
½	teaspoon ginger, sliced
1	teaspoon paprika
4	sprigs fresh cilantro, chopped
4	medium onions, sliced (2 cups)
1	cup sliced ripe tomato
¼	cup light beer
2	teaspoons red wine vinegar
2	tablespoons water
1	teaspoon salt, or to taste
2	pounds fillets of flounder or similar fish, cut into 8 pieces

1. Heat the oil in a large skillet. Add the garlic, ginger, and paprika and stir-fry a moment to combine. Add the cilantro, onions, and tomato and stir-fry over moderate heat for 2 minutes.

2. Add the beer, vinegar, and water and stir to combine. Push the mixture to the side and place the fish pieces on the bottom of the skillet. Top with the onion/tomato mixture. Cover the skillet and cook over low heat for 10 minutes.

Serve warm, with rice or boiled yuca. **Serves 8**

Pango de Pescado con Platano (Iquitos)

FISH AND PLANTAINS

Paiche *is the fish of choice in this jungle-style fish preparation. The much admired* paiche *is an enormous fish of the Amazon River; some of them, my informants tell me, are six feet long. The ones I saw in the public market were indeed very large and desirable. Some of the other fish from the "black water lakes" that abound near the Amazon and its tributaries are positively Neolithic—small, misshapen, black—yet attractive to local cooks.*

Note that you can use ripe plantains—the ones with the yellow/black skin (which I prefer because they are sweeter)—or the hard green ones, which must be cooked longer.

2	pounds fillets of *paiche*, or substitute flounder, red snapper, or similar fish, cut into 6 pieces
2	teaspoons salt
3	plantains, preferably ripe ones with yellow/black skin, peeled
3	cups water
¼	cup chopped sweet red pepper
I	small onion, chopped (⅓ cup)
6	sprigs fresh cilantro, chopped

1. Rinse the fish in cold water and rub with the salt. Cover and refrigerate for 24 hours.

2. Cut the plantains in half crosswise and cook in the water over moderate heat for 10 minutes to soften. Add the fish pieces, red pepper, onion, and cilantro. Cover and cook the mixture over low heat for 15 to 20 minutes.

Serve warm, with 1 piece of fish, 1 section of plantain, and the quantity of sauce desired, with rice. **Serves 6**

Sudado de Pescado (Iquitos)

FISH LAYERED WITH VEGETABLES AND GINGER

Fresh ginger does not turn up very often in Peruvian cooking unless, I believe, the recipe is linked to the Chinese. This recipe has several logical clues that reveal its source. There are the scallions, known as Chinese onions, the ginger, and the seasonings that are stir-fried. That said, it is a Peruvian recipe from the Amazon region, which only thickens the plot.

2	tablespoons corn oil
3	cloves garlic, chopped
½	teaspoon turmeric
¼	teaspoon cumin
¼	teaspoon pepper
2	pounds fish, such as sea bass, red snapper, or similar fish, cut into 8 pieces
1	large onion (1 pound), sliced ¼-inch thick (1½ cups)
1	sweet red pepper, sliced into julienne strips (1 cup)
1½	cups sliced ripe tomatoes (2 medium)
1	teaspoon salt, or to taste
	A ½-inch piece fresh ginger, peeled and crushed
¼	cup water
2	scallions, sliced thin

1. Heat the oil in a large shallow pan and stir-fry the garlic, turmeric, cumin, and pepper over low heat for 2 minutes.

2. Arrange the fish pieces on top and fry for 2 minutes.

3. Spread a layer of the onion over the fish; top with a layer of the red pepper, then a layer of tomatoes, and season with the salt. Add the ginger. Cover the pan and cook for 10 minutes.

4. Add the water and simmer for 10 minutes more to allow sauce to accumulate, basting the layers several times with the pan juices. Sprinkle the scallions over all, cover the pan, and let stand off the heat for 5 minutes before serving.

Serve warm with rice. **Serves 8**

Mazamorra de Pescado con Platano (Iquitos)

FISH AND PLANTAIN MELANGE

The tropical climate of the Amazon region provides the enormous freshwater fish called paiche *and plantains, both called for in this recipe. All of the ingredients of this essentially jungle food dish are to be found locally. The river people of Iquitos virtually live off the land—as it should be.*

10	sprigs fresh cilantro, sliced, plus 1 tablespoon chopped
1	large onion, sliced (1 cup)
1	large sweet green or red pepper, sliced (1 cup)
4	cloves garlic, sliced
8	cups (2 quarts) water
6	green plantains, peeled and grated by hand or in a processor
2	pounds *paiche* (as used by Amazonian cooks) or substitute red snapper, sea bass, or a similar sea fish cut into 8 pieces
2	teaspoons salt, or to taste
¼	teaspoon cumin
¼	cup corn oil
1	teaspoon turmeric
¼	cup chopped tomato
¼	cup chopped onion

1. In a food processor, process the cilantro sprigs, onion slices, sweet pepper, and garlic to a smooth paste with ¼ cup water. Set aside.

2. Bring the water to a boil in a large pan. Squeeze the grated plantain through a towel to remove excess liquid and add it to the water. Stir continuously over low heat for 20 minutes. Add the fish and salt. Stir in the garlic/cilantro paste mixture and cumin. Stir well, cover, and simmer for 20 minutes.

3. Heat the oil in a large skillet and stir-fry the turmeric, tomato, and chopped onion over low heat for 3 minutes. Stir into the fish mixture. Sprinkle with chopped cilantro.

Serve warm. **Serves 8**

Caigua con Relleno de Pescado (Lambayeque)

FISH-STUFFED CAIGUA

Caigua is the odd, twisted-shaped green gourd with a hollow center that is found all over Peru. I have not yet discovered its botanical history. From a culinary point of view, Peruvians empty the vegetable of seeds and veins and fill it with fish or chicken stuffing. It is popular with families and ubiquitous in public markets.

Since caigua is not, to my knowledge, available in New York, Peruvians have suggested that sweet red or green peppers can be legitimately substituted.

THE STUFFING

8	medium sweet red or green peppers
2	cups water
1	pound fish fillets, such as flounder, red snapper, or a similar fish; cut into 1-inch cubes
4	slices white bread, crusts removed, and moistened with milk (to make 1 cup)
1	egg, beaten
1	medium onion, sliced thin (½ cup)
½	teaspoon salt

¼   **teaspoon pepper**

THE BROTH SAUCE

1   **tablespoon corn oil**

¼   **cup sliced onion**

¼   **cup chopped tomato**

¼   **teaspoon paprika**

2   **cloves garlic, ground to a paste with
2 tablespoons water**

1   **cup reserved fish broth**

1. Cut out a 2-inch round from the top of each pepper and remove the core and seeds. Set aside.

2. Make the stuffing: Bring the water to a boil. Add the fish fillets, cover the pan, and simmer over low heat for 10 minutes. Remove the fish and cool. Reserve 1 cup broth. Pull the cubes apart into threads. In a bowl mix the fish threads with the moistened bread and add the egg, onion, salt, and pepper, mixing well.

3. Make the broth sauce: Heat the oil in a skillet. Add the onion, tomato, paprika, and garlic paste and stir-fry over low heat for 3 minutes. Add the 1 cup reserved fish broth and bring to a boil.

4. Fill the peppers with the fish stuffing and replace the tops. (Should there be any stuffing left over, shape egg-sized fish balls and set aside.)

5. Place the stuffed peppers in the broth sauce (with any fish balls from any leftover stuffing). Simmer, covered, over low heat for 15 minutes.

Serve hot, with rice. **Serves 8**

Special Note: The same stuffing may be used to prepare egg-shaped balls, Albondigas de Pescado. Cook in 1 cup of either fish or chicken broth for the time indicated in the recipe. Serve with rice. Serves 8.

Bacalao (Chincha)

SALT FISH STEW FOR EASTER

It is traditional among the Negroes of Chincha to refrain from eating meat and concentrate on fish during Easter (Semana Santa). Bacalao is one of the popular dishes during this holy time. Both cod and sea bass are salted during the season when the fish, especially cod, are plentiful.

2	pounds *bacalao* (dried salted cod)
2	tablespoons corn oil
2	cloves garlic, ground to a paste with 2 tablespoons water
I	pound onions (2 or 3), coarsely chopped
I	pound ripe tomato, coarsely chopped
I	tablespoon tomato paste, for color
2	bay leaves
¼	teaspoon pepper
¼	teaspoon ground cumin
3	potatoes (I pound), peeled, cooked, and quartered
I	sweet red pepper, cut into long slices
I	sweet green pepper, cut into long slices
½	cup fresh or frozen green peas
½	cup diced carrot

1. Cover the *bacalao* with cold water and soak overnight. Change the water twice during this time. Drain. Pull the soft, moist fish into shreds 2 to 3 inches long. Set aside.

2. Heat the oil in a pan. Add the garlic and onions and stir-fry over low heat for 1 minute. Add the tomato, tomato paste, and bay leaves. Stir-fry to combine.

3. Add the *bacalao*, pepper, cumin, potatoes, red and green peppers, peas, and carrot. Stir-fry over low heat for 10 minutes to integrate all the flavors.

Serve warm, with white wine. **Serves 8 to 10**

Calamar Relleno (Chincha)

STUFFED SQUID

*Squid are stuffed with some of the recognizable ingredients
of Peru, like* queso fresco *and* huacatay, *with its floral-like aroma.
Medium-size squid, about 6 inches long, cleaned, make a good size to
stuff. Allow one per person, as an unconventional appetizer.*

1	tablespoon *huacatay* (see Glossary)
2	cloves garlic, chopped
1	tablespoon olive oil
1	large onion, chopped (1 cup)
1	cup fresh or frozen green peas
1	cup carrot, cut into ¼-inch dice
¼	teaspoon salt, or to taste
⅛	teaspoon pepper
1	cup diced *queso fresco* (see Glossary) or Feta cheese
6	medium squid, cleaned
2	tablespoons butter
6	lettuce leaves
6	lemon or lime wedges
¼	cup corn oil
4	potatoes (1 pound) cooked in skins, peeled, and cut into rounds

1. In a blender or food processor, process the *huacatay* and garlic to a smooth paste with ¼ cup water. Set aside.

2. Heat the olive oil in a large skillet. Add the onion, garlic paste, peas, carrot, salt, and pepper, and stir-fry for 2 minutes. Stir in the *queso fresco* until combined. Let cool, then stuff each squid completely.

3. Rub a baking pan with the butter. Arrange the stuffed squid in the pan and bake in a preheated 350 degree oven for 15 to 20 minutes.

4. While the squid bakes, heat the corn oil. Add the potato slices and fry, turning, until crisp.

5. To serve, arrange the serving platter as follows: On one end, make a fan with the lettuce leaves, then put the lemon wedges over it. On the other end, arrange the fried potatoes. In the center, put the squid.

Serve at room temperature, as an appetizer. **Serves 6**

Tortilla de Raya (Santa Rosa)
STINGRAY PANCAKE

The venomous stingray has two edible wings that are popular as a foodstuff with Asian communities and in those areas where they are caught. Stingray is an exotic seafood available in New York's Chinatown. Those that are caught in the northern waters off the coast of Peru are turned into a pancake by the local restaurants along the seaboard.

2	**pounds stingray wings**
3	**scallions, sliced thin**
¼	**teaspoon pepper**
¼	**cup flour**
5	**eggs, beaten**
¼	**cup corn oil**

1. Cook the ray, covered, in water over moderate heat for 15 minutes. Remove and cool. Discard the liquid. Pull the cooked ray apart into strips and discard all the bones.

2. In a bowl mix together well the shredded ray, scallions, pepper, flour, and eggs.

3. Heat the oil in a wok or skillet. Add the ray mixture and fry over low heat for 2 to 3 minutes on each side. Remove and drain briefly on paper towels.

Serve as an appetizer, with *Zarza* (page 204). **Serves 4**

Trucha Atomatada (Puno)

BAKED TROUT IN TOMATO SAUCE

A popular and doable method of cooking fresh trout from the waters of Peru.

½	cup peeled chopped tomato
¼	cup water
2	tablespoons corn oil
2	cloves garlic, ground to a paste with 2 tablespoons water
I	small onion, crushed
I	teaspoon salt
⅛	teaspoon pepper
¼	teaspoon sugar
	A I¼-pound whole fresh trout, cleaned
2	tablespoons red wine
3	sprigs parsley, chopped

1. In a food processor process the tomato to a paste with the water.

2. Heat the oil in a skillet. Add the garlic paste and onion and stir-fry over low heat for 2 minutes. Add the tomato paste, salt, pepper, and sugar and mix to combine and warm through.

3. Put the trout in an oiled Pyrex baking dish and pour the wine over it. Cover with the prepared tomato sauce and sprinkle the parsley over it. Bake in a preheated 350 degree oven for 20 minutes.

Serve warm, with hot rice, boiled potatoes, or mixed vegetables.
Serves 2

Trucha Rellena (Puno)

STUFFED TROUT

The rivers and lakes of Peru are stocked with trout, and this is in addition to the wild variety, which provides a mixture of genes—another topic. Here is an admirable preparation, and all of the ingredients are available to the cooks in the United States. Try it, you will like it.

½	teaspoon salt
⅛	teaspoon pepper
	A 1-pound whole fresh trout, cleaned, head and tail included
3	or 4 little-finger-sized pieces *queso fresco* (see Glossary) or Feta cheese
3	or 4 little-finger-sized pieces boiled ham
2	tablespoons flour
1	egg, beaten
3	tablespoons plain dry bread crumbs
¼	cup corn oil

1. Salt and pepper the inside of the trout. Add the pieces of cheese and ham, enough to fill the cavity. Press to close.

2. Dredge the trout in the flour, then dip it into the egg, coating it on all around. Roll in the bread crumbs.

3. Heat the oil in a large skillet and fry the trout over moderate heat for about 4 minutes on each side. Drain on paper towels.

Serve warm, with crisp French fries. **Serves 4**

Hueveras Fritas (Huanchaco)

FRIED FISH ROE

Huanchaco is the beach that extends from the city of Trujillo. Fish is plentiful there, and during the season fish roe is available. When fried, fish roe has the tendency to splatter now and then, like corn when it pops. It is prudent, therefore, to partially cover the skillet while cooking roe.

½ pound fish roe, such as flounder, mackerel, or other
   popular fish (available in season)
½   teaspoon salt
2   tablespoons fresh lime juice
3   tablespoons flour
¼   cup corn oil
   Lime slices, for serving

1. Rinse the roe in cold water and dry on paper towels. Sprinkle on the salt and lime juice. Dust with the flour.

2. Heat the oil in a skillet and add the roe, 1 at a time. Fry on both sides over moderately low heat for 3 to 4 minutes total cooking time. Drain on paper towels.

Serve warm, with lime slices, as an appetizer. **Serves 4**

Choro a la Criollo (Chincha)

STUFFED GREEN MUSSELS

Green mussels are imported from New Zealand and are available now fresh or frozen. The mussels are large and meaty and sometimes are packed with one of the shells removed. When frozen, they must be thawed and rinsed well in cold water before you use them.

A generous portion is calculated as 4 mussels per person as an appetizer.

24 green mussels, well rinsed

THE STUFFING

4 medium onions, chopped (2 cups)

2 cups drained canned corn niblets or frozen niblets, thawed

2 teaspoons olive oil

1 ripe medium tomato, chopped (1 cup)

½ teaspoon salt

⅛ teaspoon pepper

8 sprigs fresh cilantro, trimmed and chopped

Juice of 3 lemons

1. In a skillet steam the mussels, covered, over moderate heat in a small amount of water, about 1 cup, for 5 minutes. Drain and set aside.

2. Prepare the stuffing: Put the onions, corn, oil, tomato, salt, pepper, cilantro, and lemon juice together in a bowl and mix well.

3. Assemble the mussels on the half shell on individual plates or on a large serving platter. Cover each mussel generously with some of the onion/corn stuffing. Cover and chill.

Serve cold, as an appetizer. **Serves 6 or more**

Aji de Camarones (Arequipa)

SHRIMP WITH AJI CHILI

The aji chili when seeded is less hot than it is with seeds. Another ingredient here is huacatay, *a mysterious and effective herb of the marigold family. The only limiting factor is, as always, the freshness of the shrimp; it pays to look around.*

2	tablespoons corn oil
I	clove garlic, chopped
I	medium onion, chopped (½ cup)
⅓	cup chopped peeled tomato
I	cup Shrimp Broth (page 37)
3	pounds medium shrimp, peeled, deveined, and halved lengthwise
½	teaspoon *huacatay* (see Glossary)
2	teaspoons dry white wine
½	teaspoon salt, or to taste
4	whole peppercorns
¼	teaspoon cumin
I	teaspoon freshly chopped seeded fresh *aji amarillo* (yellow Peruvian chili, see Glossary) or I teaspoon dried *aji* yellow chili powder
I	cup diced cooked potato (¼-inch dice)
I	hard-boiled egg, peeled and sliced, for garnish

1. Heat the oil in a large skillet. Add the garlic, onion, and tomato, and stir-fry over low heat for 3 minutes.

2. Add the broth and bring to a boil. Add the shrimp and cook for 3 minutes. Add the *huacatay*, wine, salt, peppercorns, cumin, *aji* and potato. Cover and simmer over low heat for 3 minutes, stirring once or twice. Garnish with the egg slices.

Serve warm, with rice. **Serves 6 to 8**

Picante de Camarones (Chiclayo)

AJI-CHILI-SPICED SHRIMP

Although the yellow aji *chili is mild in flavor, there is enough of it in this recipe to provide a Peruvian jolt. This is an attractive dish, with a number of garnishes in Peruvian style—altogether enticing.*

1	tablespoon corn oil
¼	cup fresh or frozen green peas
1	medium sweet red pepper, seeded and chopped (1 cup)
3	fresh *aji amarillo* (yellow Peruvian chili, see Glossary), or 4 teaspoons dried yellow *aji* chili powder
2	cloves garlic, ground to a paste with 2 tablespoons water
1½	pounds medium shrimp, peeled and deveined
1	cup Shrimp or Fish Broth (page 35)
1	teaspoon *achiote* granules dissolved in 2 tablespoons hot corn oil
3	sprigs fresh cilantro, chopped fine
½	teaspoon salt
⅛	teaspoon pepper
½	cup evaporated or fresh milk
2	teaspoons cornstarch, dissolved in 2 tablespoons cold water
	Several lettuce leaves
1	large ripe tomato, sliced
2	hard-boiled eggs, peeled and sliced
6	black olives
6	large (thumb-sized) yuca pieces, peeled and cooked (see page 21 for directions)
½	cup *Zarza* (see Index)

1. Heat the oil in a pan. Add the peas, red pepper, *aji*, and garlic paste and stir-fry over low heat for 1 minute.

2. Add the shrimp, broth, cilantro, salt, and pepper and bring to a boil. Add the milk and enough of the cornstarch mixture to thicken the mixture into a smooth sauce.

3. To serve, line a large bowl with the lettuce leaves. Pour on the shrimp and sauce. Garnish with the tomato slices, egg slices, olives, and yuca. Spoon the *Zarza* over the lettuce and tomato slices.

Serve warm, with white rice. **Serves 6**

Camarones al Ajo (Chiclayo)
FRIED SHRIMP WITH GARLIC SAUCE

Garlic is the predominant flavor here since it seasons the shrimp both in a quick marinade and later in a sauce. Garlic is used frequently in Peruvian cooking. Large amounts of it called for, therefore, should not intimidate since the proof is in the eating.

THE SHRIMP

6	cloves garlic, ground to a paste with 2 tablespoons water
I	tablespoon finely chopped seeded fresh *aji amarillo* (yellow Peruvian chili, see Glossary) or I teaspoon dried yellow *aji* chili powder
⅓	cup wine or cider vinegar
¼	teaspoon salt
⅛	teaspoon pepper
I½	pounds medium shrimp, peeled and deveined
½	cup flour
⅓	cup corn oil for frying

THE GARLIC SAUCE

3	tablespoons butter
5	tablespoons ground garlic
I	cup Shrimp or Fish Broth (page 35)
I	teaspoon cornstarch, dissolved in 2 tablespoons cold water
	Tomato slices, lettuce leaves, 12 black olives
I	hard-boiled egg, peeled and sliced

1. Mix together the garlic paste, *aji*, vinegar, salt, and pepper. Add the shrimp, mix well, and let stand 5 minutes. Drain and toss the shrimp with the flour.

2. Heat the oil in a wok or skillet. Add the shrimp and stir-fry over moderate heat until crisp, about 3 minutes. Drain on paper towels.

3. Make the garlic sauce: Melt the butter in a large skillet. Add the garlic and fry over low heat for 2 minutes. Add the broth and bring to a boil. Stir in enough of the cornstarch mixture until thickened to your taste.

4. To serve, arrange the tomato slices and olives around the perimeter of a serving platter or bowl lined with the lettuce. Pour in the garlic sauce and put the crisp fried shrimp over that.

Serve warm, with rice. **Serves 6**

Chupe de Camarones
Viernes (Arequipa)

SHRIMP AND VEGETABLE STEW FOR FRIDAY

Peruvian cooks often assign dishes for certain days. In Arequipa, this chupe is prepared on Friday. It is a grand presentation, with a long list of vital ingredients. And the shrimp are always fresh because of the nearby ocean.

1	tablespoon corn oil
2	cloves garlic, chopped fine
1	small onion, chopped (⅓ cup)
1	tablespoon finely chopped seeded fresh *aji amarillo* (yellow Peruvian chili, see Glossary), seeded, chopped
¼	cup chopped tender celery heart (¼-inch pieces)
1	cup shredded cabbage
1	carrot, sliced thin (½ cup)
½	cup thinly sliced leek, white part only, rinse well
½	cup chopped green beans (½-inch pieces)
½	pound *Zapallo* (see Glossary) or butternut squash, peeled and cut into ½-inch cubes
5	small potatoes, peeled and halved (1 pound)
1	ear of corn, cut into 2-inch pieces
4	cups Fish Broth (page 35)
2	pounds medium shrimp, in the shell, well rinsed
12	small hard-shelled clams, shucked
1	cup evaporated milk
½	cup cooked rice
5	eggs, lightly fried
1	tablespoon chopped parsley, for garnish

1. Heat the oil in a large pan. Add the garlic, onion, and *aji* and stir-fry over low heat for 2 minutes. Add the celery, cabbage, carrot, leek, beans, and squash and stir-fry 2 minutes.

2. Add the potatoes, corn, and broth and cook until tender.

3. Lastly, add the shrimp and clams and simmer for 5 minutes. Add the milk and rice and simmer 2 more minutes.

To serve, put an assortment of seafood and vegetables into each serving bowl. Top with 1 lightly fried egg and garnish with the chopped parsley.

Serve hot. **Serves 5 or more**

Note: All the steps are designed so that the seafood and vegetables do not over-cook. There are 18 different ingredients. One can simplify the stew by omitting a vegetable or two without diluting the overall taste.

When Fish or Shrimp Broth is called for, either can be used, as well as a mixture of both.

Moqueguano de Camaron (Arequipa)
SHRIMP IN THE SHELL WITH SEAWEED

This is an odd combination of ingredients since Arequipa in the south is near but not on the sea. Yet it all works in a highly seasoned milk sauce. Seaweed is known as yuyo *and harvested in the Pacific. The cooking in northern Peru also features* yuyo *in seafood dishes. It is possible to find fresh seaweed in both Korean and Japanese markets.*

1	tablespoon plus 2 teaspoons corn oil
1	small onion, chopped (⅓ cup)
2	cloves garlic, mashed
1	teaspoon paprika
½	teaspoon salt, or to taste
¼	teaspoon cumin
1	to 1½ pounds medium shrimp in the shell
1	teaspoon flour
½	cup shelled fresh fava beans, cooked
1	ear of corn cooked, and kernels cut off (about ⅔ cup)
3	whole potatoes (1 pound), cooked, peeled, and quartered
½	cup yuyo (fresh seaweed, see Glossary)
¼	cup evaporated milk or ½ cup fresh milk
¼	cup cubed mozzarella cheese
1	teaspoon *huacatay* (see Glossary)

1. Heat the 1 tablespoon oil in a large pan. Add the onion, garlic, paprika, salt, and cumin and stir-fry over low heat for 3 minutes.

2. Separately, heat the 2 teaspoons oil over moderate heat, add the shrimp, sprinkle the flour over them, and fry for 3 minutes. Add the shrimp to the garlic mixture.

3. Add the fava beans, corn, and potatoes to the pan. Stir in the seaweed, milk, cheese, and *huacatay* and stir-fry for 2 minutes to combine.

Serve hot, with rice. **Serves 6 to 8**

Ocopa de Camarones (Arequipa)
SPICY SHRIMP PASTE WITH POTATOES

This is an odd but attractive get-together of shrimp, peanuts, cheese,
huacatay, *yellow* aji *chili, and potatoes. Of course, potatoes.*
What would one do without them in Peru?

2	tablespoons corn oil
1	pound medium shrimp, peeled and deveined
3	cloves garlic, chopped
1	medium onion, chopped (½ cup)
5	teaspoons dried yellow *aji* chili powder (see Glossary)
2	tablespoons dry roasted peanuts
2	tablespoons grated Parmesan cheese
1	teaspoon salt, or to taste
½	teaspoon *huacatay* (see Glossary)
6	small whole potatoes, (1½ pounds) boiled and peeled

1. Heat the oil in a skillet, add the shrimp, and stir-fry over low heat for 2 minutes. Cool a minute, then cut off ⅓ of the tail end of the

shrimp. Separate the thick bodies and tails of the shrimp into 2 piles.

2. In the same oil in the skillet stir-fry the garlic and onion over low heat for 2 minutes. Remove.

3. In a food processor process the larger body sections of shrimp to a coarse paste. Add the chili powder, garlic and onion mixture, peanuts, cheese, salt, and *huacatay* for a minute, until relatively smooth.

Serve the shrimp paste over the 6 whole potatoes and garnish with the tail ends of the shrimp.

Serve warm or room temperature. **Serves 6**

Marisco Saltado con Pescado y Hongos (Peruvian/Japanese)

SHELLFISH STIR-FRY WITH FISH AND MUSHROOMS

This melange of seafood is Japanese inspired, with sesame oil, soy sauce, and oyster sauce lending the Asian touch.

¼	cup corn oil
1	tablespoon chopped garlic
1	teaspoon chopped ginger
1	cup medium shrimp, peeled and deveined
1	cup 2-inch thin slices fillets of flounder or similar fish
1	cup squid rings
1	cup whole small scallops
3	ounces dried mushrooms (allow 5 per person)
2	large sweet red or green peppers, cut into long thin slices
1	large onion, cut into long slices (1 cup)
1	cup celery heart slices (cut on the diagonal)
½	teaspoon sugar
¼	cup soy sauce
¼	cup oyster sauce
1	teaspoon sesame oil
½	cup Fish Broth (page 35)
½	teaspoon cornstarch, dissolved in 2 tablespoons water

1. Heat the corn oil in a wok or large skillet. Add the garlic and ginger and stir-fry over high heat for 1 minute. Add all the seafood (a total of 3 pounds shrimp, fish, squid, and scallops) and stir-fry for 5 minutes.

2. Remove the seafood with a strainer to a bowl and set aside. Add the mushrooms, red or green peppers, onion, celery, sugar, soy sauce, oyster sauce, and sesame oil and combine. Stir in the fish broth. Quickly

stir in the cornstarch mix, fold in the reserved seafood, and remove the pan from the heat. (The vegetables must be very lightly cooked, so speed is essential at the end to prevent them from overcooking.)

Serve hot with white rice. **Serves 6 to 8**

Arroz con Mariscos (Lima)
SEAFOOD AND RICE

It is logical that seafood be cooked with rice in a one-dish meal. The fresh scallops, shrimp, squid and octopus used here are always available in certain parts of Peru, drawn as they are from a plentiful sea. Be sure to prepare all the seafood ingredients in advance to make finishing this dish easy.

1	tablespoon corn oil
2	cloves garlic, chopped fine
1	small onion, chopped (¼ cup)
1	small tomato, chopped (¼ cup)
2	teaspoons tomato paste
½	cup scallops, halved and stir-fried for 1 minute
½	cup shrimp, peeled, deveined, halved, and stir-fried for 1 minute
½	cup sliced squid, blanched in boiling water for 1 minute
½	cup octopus, cooked in boiling water for 1 hour, or until tender, and sliced thin
1	teaspoon dried yellow *aji* chili powder (see **Glossary**)
2	tablespoons white wine
4	cups (1 quart) water
2	cups rice
1	teaspoon salt, or to taste

Heat the oil in a pan and add the garlic, onion, tomato, and tomato paste and stir fry over moderate heat for 2 minutes. Add the cooked seafood, chili powder, white wine, and water and bring to a boil. Add the rice and salt and bring to a boil again. Reduce the heat to low. Simmer the mixture for 15 minutes, enough to cook the rice and integrate all the flavors.

Serve warm, garnished with the scallop shells, if you have them. **Serves 6 or 7**

Chicharón Mixto de Mariscos (Huanchaco)

CRISPY FRIED MIXED SEAFOOD

Huanchaco is the seaside resort for the people of Trujillo who throng there on weekends and public holidays. One of the popular dishes in this town on the northern coastline of Peru is this deep-fried assortment of seafood freshly harvested from the sea.

1	**cup sliced fresh squid (½-inch rounds)**
1	**cup salt water shrimp, peeled and deveined**
½	**cup freshwater shrimp, peeled (optional)**
3	**or 4 fish roe (available in season)**
1	**cup cooked octopus, sliced ¼-inch thick (see Note, page 103)**
1	**teaspoon salt**
½	**teaspoon cumin**
3	**cloves garlic, crushed**
¼	**teaspoon pepper**
1	**cup flour**
1	**cup corn oil**
	Lettuce leaves, for serving
	Tomato slices, for serving
	Cucumber slices, for serving

1. Blanch the squid, shrimp, and fish roe in boiling water for 10 seconds. (Octopus is tough and must be cooked in water for about 1 hour before slicing.) Drain and cool. Transfer to a large bowl.

2. Add salt, cumin, garlic, and pepper to the seafood. Toss with the flour.

3. Heat the oil in a wok or large skillet over moderate heat. Add the seafood, a few pieces at a time, and fry, turning for 3 or 4 minutes. Remove and drain on paper towels.

Line a serving platter with the lettuce leaves and put the tomato and cucumber slices around the perimeter. Top with the warm seafood.

Serve warm, with your favorite *Zarza* (see Index). **Serves 8, as an appetizer**

Chupe de Mariscos de Huanchaco

SEAFOOD STEW FROM HUANCHACO

The beach of the Huanchaco, not too far from the northern city of Trujillo, is long and wide and filled with the artifacts of a sea-going community. Handmade reed boats lean against sea walls or can be seen being carried to the shore by muscular fishermen. And, of course, there are seafood restaurants all over the place that produce traditional fish dishes of fine quality and quantity. Peruvians like to eat!

4	cups (1 quart) water
½	pound octopus, cooked (see Note) and sliced
½	pound snails, very well rinsed
½	pound small shrimp in the shell
½	pound crab (5 or 6), top shell removed and discarded
8	mussels, rinsed
½	teaspoon salt
½	cup chopped tomato
3	cloves garlic, chopped fine
½	cup chopped onion
2	teaspoons dried oregano
1	cup fresh or frozen green peas
8	hard-boiled eggs, peeled
2	cups evaporated or fresh milk or half-and-half
2	tablespoons butter
1	cup cooked rice

1. Bring the water to a boil in a large pan. Add the octopus, snails, shrimp, crabs, and mussels and simmer, covered, over moderate heat for 10 minutes.

2. Add the salt, tomato, garlic, onion, oregano, peas, and eggs and simmer over low heat for 5 minutes. Finally, add the milk, butter, and rice and simmer 10 minutes more.

Serve hot. **Serves 8**

Note: Octopus is very firm-fleshed and requires cooking for about 1 hour in boiling water before it is ready to be included in seafood stews or soups. Drain, then slice and use.

Tortilla de Mariscos (Callao)

ASSORTED SEAFOOD OMELET

In my opinion, this is one of the all-time best omelets that can be served for brunch or lunch, hot or cold.

¾	cup squid, sliced into thin rounds
¼	cup thinly sliced cooked octopus (see Note, page 103)
½	cup small shrimp, peeled and deveined
6	small scallops, halved
6	eggs, lightly beaten
¼	cup chopped onion
1	tablespoon chopped sweet red pepper
2	tablespoons green peas
2	tablespoons diced carrot
2	teaspoons chopped fresh cilantro
¼	teaspoon dried oregano
1	teaspoon salt, or to taste
⅛	teaspoon pepper
1	clove garlic, crushed
1	tablespoon flour
¼	cup olive oil

1. Put the seafood, eggs, onion, red pepper, peas, carrot, cilantro, oregano, salt, pepper, garlic, and flour in a bowl and mix together well.

2. Heat the oil in a large skillet. Add the omelet mixture and fry over low heat for 3 minutes. Cover the skillet with a flat lid or a large plate

and turn the omelet over onto the lid or plate. Then slide the omelet carefully back into the skillet and brown for 3 more minutes.

Serve hot, with salsa criolla (page 204). **Serves 6**

Saltado de Mariscos (Chincha)

ASSORTED STIR-FRIED SEAFOOD

A saltado *is a popular method of cooking meats and seafood.
In my opinion, it appears to be of Chinese technique, with a Peruvian slant, indicated by the crisp French fries that are folded into the prepared dish to provide bulk and flavor. A splash of wine vinegar also adds more dimension to the seafood and vegetables.*

2	pounds medium shrimp, peeled, deveined, and halved lengthwise
1	pound young octopus, cooked and cut into thin slices (see Note, page 103)
2	pounds squid, cut into 1/2-inch-wide round slices
1	pound scallops, sliced
½	teaspoon salt
¼	teaspoon pepper
2	cloves garlic, ground to a paste with 2 tablespoons water
3	tablespoons corn oil
2	large onions, sliced thin (2 cups)
1	large sweet red pepper, cut into thin slices
2	large tomatoes, sliced into little-finger-sized strips (2 cups)
1½	pounds potatoes, cooked as crisp French fries (see Step 2, page 28)
6	sprigs fresh cilantro, chopped
2	tablespoons distilled wine vinegar

1. In a bowl combine the shrimp, octopus, squid, and scallops with the salt, pepper, and garlic paste. Set aside.

2. Heat the oil in a wok or large skillet. Add the seafood and stir-fry over moderate heat for 4 minutes.

3. Add the onions, red pepper, and tomatoes and stir-fry for 2 minutes. Fold in the French fries, cilantro, and vinegar, stirring to combine well for 2 minutes more. Adjust the salt if necessary.

Serve warm. **Serves 6 to 8**

Note: If you live near a Korean supermarket, you will be able to find already cooked young octopus. Simply slice it into ½-inch-wide rounds. If you need to cook the octopus, purchase and cook the tentacles until tender, at least ½ hour in water to cover. Drain and slice into rounds.

IŮS
COMOLEQVITAALPOBRE.

Giego su carnero para el tributo el mandon Mayamuy taza macho

manam tazayoc
chocani pazasca
nachum chacuay
camalica llumay
ca machuypa ya
yay pasa quisca
mi resta mento
pi saquiuan

enbidia   q̃alos

BEEF, PORK, LAMB, AND OTHER MEATS

Peru is a poor country with a very rich ethnic history. Meat is money in a poor place, and Peruvian cooks know how to stretch meat to interminable lengths. For example, in Loma a lo Pobre (Steak for the Poor), one pound of steak is supplemented with French fries, plantains, fried eggs, one pound each of tomatoes and onions, plus vivid seasonings. This will serve six to eight persons. In the frigid Andean highlands, Adobo de Chancho (Pork in a Thick Sauce) is equally filling, with hot chilies, potatoes, and enough garlic to ward off a vampire.

Exotic meats such as alpaca, deer meat from the Amazon region, and the beloved if not notorious guinea pig (*cuy*) are found in regional markets. In one market town, two Quechua Incas in their white stovepipe hats were discussing in Spanish the evils of cholesterol and noting that alpaca is not only the cheapest meat but very low in cholesterol.

Peruvians are big eaters and home cooks must fill family stomachs, always realizing that there are many enticing ways to prepare meat dishes in their region. One reason a recipe evolves is because there is a need to provide sustenance for a large family. Later, more sophisticated ingredients and combinations are added, which convert a particular dish from one for mere *eating* to one to *dine on*.

Meats, especially, qualify for this type of culinary modification.

Espesado de Lunes (Chiclayo)

BEEF, THE THICKENING OF MONDAYS

This is a special dish that is only prepared on Mondays. My teacher told me that everyone she knew cooked Espesado on Mondays, a ritual that is universally accepted. In the clean and complete Central Market of Chiclayo, a number of the small eating shops were dispensing this to diners who knew what they wanted and expected it on Mondays.

THE MUSH

2	pounds fresh or frozen corn kernels (*choclo*)
½	cup *Zapallo* (see Glossary) or butternut squash, cut into ¼-inch dice
6	sprigs fresh cilantro, sliced
6	cloves garlic, sliced
I	small onion, sliced (¼ cup)
⅔	cup water

THE MEAT

4	cups (I quart) water
2	pounds boneless beef brisket or chuck, cut into 16 pieces
I	teaspoon salt, or to taste
½	pound yuca (see Glossary), peeled and cut into ¼-inch dice
½	pound shelled fresh fava beans (optional, but traditional)

1. To make the mush: Process all the ingredients together in a food processor into a fine paste or mush. Set aside.

2. To prepare the meat: Bring the water to a boil in a large pan. Add the beef, salt, yuca, and fava beans (if used) and simmer, covered, over low heat until the meat is tender, about 45 minutes.

3. Add the mush, mix well, and cook for 15 to 20 minutes. (This results in a thick and substantial dish, perhaps even too thick, in which case ½ to 1 cup water may be added.) Mix well and adjust the salt to taste.

Serve warm, with a side dish of *Ceviche* (see Glossary). **Serves 8**

Note: The original type of squash added to this dish is known locally in Chiclayo as *loche*. It is long, about 14 inches, knobby, and unattractive-looking and is seen in the markets there, but nowhere else, to my experience. The Chiclayanos swear by it as being indispensable to *espesado*, but in my opinion this has more to do with chauvinism than with culinary excellence.

Loma Saltado (Trujillo)

BEEF FILLET WITH VEGETABLE SAUCE

*Here is a filling dish of beef (not too much) and French fries
(not greasy) combined with fresh yellow aji (also known as* escabeche),
which provides color and a moderately hot touch.

1	**cup corn oil, for deep-frying**
2	**pounds large potatoes, peeled and cut into French-fry-sized pieces**
1	**pound beef fillet, cut into little-finger-sized slices**
1	**clove garlic, chopped**
½	**cup sliced onion**
¼	**teaspoon cumin**
½	**teaspoon salt, or to taste**
2	**teaspoons red wine vinegar**
¼	**cup chopped fresh tomato**
1	**fresh *aji amarillo* (yellow Peruvian chili, see Glossary), seeded and cut into thin slices, or 1 teaspoon dried yellow *aji* chili powder**

1. In a wok or skillet heat the oil over moderate heat until hot. Add the potatoes carefully and French-fry them. Drain on paper towels and set aside. Carefully pour off all but 1 tablespoon of the oil.

2. Combine the beef, garlic, onion, cumin, salt, and vinegar. Heat the oil in the wok or skillet, add the beef, and cook over low heat for 5 minutes, tossing.

3. Add the tomato and *aji* and fold in the French fries. Combine gently, frying the *saltado* for 2 minutes. Serve immediately

Serve warm, with rice. **Serves 6**

Asado Carne de Res (Chincha)

BEEF POT ROAST

A vinegar marinade with spices is made to penetrate a slab of beef. Then, two deep incisions are cut into the meat. One is stuffed with a whole carrot; the other with a stalk of celery. The roast is cooked slowly on top of the stove so that all of the seasonings take effect. The Negro community of Chincha knows how to cook.

⅔   cup wine vinegar

1   tablespoon salt, or to taste

⅛   teaspoon pepper

¼   teaspoon cumin

2   teaspoons paprika

5   cloves garlic, ground to a paste with
     2 tablespoons water

3   pounds beef rump steak or another
     equivalent cut of meat, in 1 piece

1   stalk celery heart

1   whole thin carrot, peeled

3   tablespoons corn oil

2   cups water

2   carrots, cut into ¼-inch dice (1 cup)

1. In a wide bowl mix together the vinegar, salt, pepper, cumin, paprika, and garlic paste. Add the beef and rub the mixture all over it. Remove the beef, reserving the marinade.

2. Cut 2 deep incisions horizontally into the meat, a few inches apart. Put the stalk of celery into one and the carrot into the other.

3. Heat the oil in a pan and brown the beef on all sides over low heat for 5 minutes. Add the vinegar mixture, water, and diced carrot, cover, and cook for about 45 minutes, or until the juice runs clear when a fork is plunged into the beef. (If the meat is too firm, then continue to cook it, covered, until tender.)

To serve, cut in generous slices so that the celery and carrot are visible in each serving. Serve warm, with white rice and a simple salad.
Serves 6 to 8

Lomo Saltado (Cuzco)

BEEF STEAK STIR-FRY

Here is a popular and ubiquitous dish that is easily assembled and seems to be of European heritage, but is made with Chinese cooking techniques. At a restaurant in Lima that became my hangout, loma saltado was served on Tuesdays, and one could count on à la carte service.

1	cup corn oil, for deep-frying
1	pound potatoes, peeled and cut into French-fry-sized pieces
1	pound tender beef steak, cut of your choice, such as sirloin or fillet, cut into 1-inch cubes
1	large onion, cut into strips like the French fries (1 cup)
1	large ripe tomato, sliced into rounds, then halved
1	teaspoon salt, or to taste
¼	teaspoon pepper
½	teaspoon dried oregano

1. In a wok or skillet heat the oil over moderate heat until hot. Add the potatoes carefully and French-fry them until crisp and brown. Drain on paper towels and set aside.

2. Carefully pour off all but 1 tablespoon of the oil. Heat the oil in the wok or skillet, add the steak cubes, and stir-fry them over moderate heat for 2 minutes. Add the onion, tomato, salt, pepper, and oregano and continue to stir-fry for 2 minutes.

3. Add the French fries, mixing them in gently but well and heat for 2 minutes.

Serve hot, with rice. **Serves 6**

Lomo a lo Pobre (Callao)

STEAK FOR THE POOR

This recipe is characterized by a lot of food in generous quantity, but utilizes only one pound of steak for six servings; French fries, fried plantains, a pound each of onions and tomatoes, and six fresh eggs top it all off. Peruvians have large appetites and prepare generous servings; Lomo a lo Pobre serves as a good example of this.

6	eggs
2	ripe plantains, yellow/black skin
1	pound rump or flank steak, cut into pieces 1 inch long by ¼ inch thick
4	cloves garlic, ground to a paste with 2 tablespoons water
1	teaspoon salt, or to taste
⅛	teaspoon pepper
2	tablespoons corn oil, plus additional oil for cooking eggs and plantains
1	pound tomatoes, sliced

I	pound onions, sliced
4	sprigs fresh cilantro, chopped fine
2	tablespoons soy sauce
I	tablespoon red wine vinegar
I	pound potatoes, French fried (see Step 2, page 28)
	Hot cooked rice; for serving

1. Fry 1 egg for each person and set aside on a large serving platter, placing them in upper right section. Peel the plantains, cut in half lengthwise, and halved again, 4 pieces. Fry in hot oil over low heat until brown and soft. Drain on paper towels.

2. Combine the steak, garlic, salt, and pepper together. In a wok or skillet heat 2 tablespoons of the oil over moderate heat. Add the beef mixture and stir-fry it for 1 minute.

3. Add the tomatoes, onions, and cilantro and stir-fry the mixture for 5 minutes. Add the soy sauce and vinegar and toss to combine.

4. Arrange the different components of this dish as follows: Place the French fries in the center of the platter. Put the fried plantains directly below the eggs on the right side of the platter. Diagonally across from the eggs, on the lower left of the platter, place hot cooked rice. Lastly, in the 11 o'clock position, place the meat mixture with its sauce. The components may also be arranged on individual plates in the same design.

Serve at once. **Serves 6**

Seca de Carne (Chincha)

BEEF STEW IN CILANTRO SAUCE

*This is much more than a stew. The power of the cilantro,
beef, and turmeric makes for a sauce that colors the stew and provides
a potent aroma. In addition, Seco is known as a combinado, or
combination, as it is served with a separate dish of Yellow Bean Stew
or plain cooked yuca. Those are the rules of the game.*

3	tablespoons corn oil
2	cloves garlic, ground to a paste with 2 tablespoons water
1	medium onion, chopped (½ cup)
2	pounds rump steak or boneless chuck, cut into 2½-inch pieces
1	teaspoon salt, or to taste
⅛	teaspoon pepper
⅛	teaspoon cumin
½	teaspoon turmeric
3	cups water
½	cup beer
4-5	ounces fresh cilantro, trimmed
1	pound yuca (see **Glossary**), peeled, cut into 8 pieces, cooked until soft, and drained
½	pound (1 cup) dried yellow beans (see **Note**)

1. Heat the oil in a pan. Add the garlic and onion and stir-fry over low heat for 1 minute. Add the beef and stir-fry for 5 minutes.

2. Add the salt, pepper, cumin, turmeric, water, and beer and bring to a boil.

3. Grind the cilantro into a smooth paste with 1/2 cup water in a food processor and add it to the beef mixture. Mix well, cover the pan, and simmer for 45 minutes, or a bit more to tenderize the beef and create a sauce with substantial flavor.

Serve warm, with either the cooked yuca or Sopa de Frijal (page 141).
Serves 6 to 8

Note: Yellow beans are imported from Peru and can be found in grocery stores that sell esoteric Peruvian foods. The beans are like any dried white supermarket bean except that they are about the same color as dried chick peas and have rounded ends.

Dried white beans are a legitimate substitute.

Rocoto Belleno (Arequipa)

STUFFED-PERUVIAN ROCOTO

The rocoto is a large chili of moderate heat that resembles the red or green supermarket sweet (bell) peppers. When the seeds and veins in the inside of the rocoto are removed, it becomes usable for stuffing. Since rocotos are not available, to my knowledge, sweet red peppers are a legitimate substitute.

THE STUFFING

- 3 tablespoons corn oil
- 1 teaspoon finely chopped seeded *aji amarillo* (Yellow Peruvian chili, see Glossary) or ½ teaspoon dried yellow *aji* chili powder
- 1 pound boneless sirloin steak or fillet, cut into ¼-inch dice
- 1 teaspoon salt
- ¼ teaspoon pepper
- 3 cloves garlic, ground to a paste with 2 tablespoons water
- 1 teaspoon dried oregano
- ¾ cup water
- 1 medium onion, chopped (½ cup)
- 1½ tablespoons ketchup
- ¼ cup dry roasted peanuts, chopped, but not too fine

6	rocotos (see introduction to recipe)
2	hard-boiled eggs, peeled and sliced into rounds
6	potatoes (1¼ pounds), peeled and cooked
½	pound mozzarella cheese, sliced into 12 pieces, each ¼ inch thick
2	eggs, beaten
2	cups evaporated or fresh milk

1. Prepare the stuffing: Heat 2 tablespoons of the oil in a skillet. Add the *aji*, beef, salt, pepper, garlic paste, and oregano and stir-fry over low heat for 3 minutes. Add the water and bring to a boil.

2. Stir-fry the onion separately in the remaining 1 tablespoon oil over low heat until golden. Stir in the ketchup and peanuts, then fold mixture into the beef mixture.

3. Bring 6 cups water to a boil in a large pan. Drop in the *rocotos* and boil for 2 minutes to rinse and soften. Drain well.

4. Stuff the *rocotos*: Cut off ½ inch from the top of each pepper and reserve. Scoop out and discard the seeds and veins, which will substantially reduce the spice heat. Rinse well with cold water. Stuff each pepper to the top with stuffing. Add 1 slice of egg and cover with the reserved top. Cover each cooked potato, all of the same size, with 1 slice of cheese.

5. Beat the eggs with 1 cup of the milk together in a food processor. Put in a skillet and simmer with ½ teaspoon salt over low heat to the consistency of scrambled eggs.

6. Place the stuffed peppers and the potatoes in a roasting pan in separate areas. Scatter the scrambled eggs over the top and pour 1 cup milk all over. Cover the potatoes and peppers with 1 slice cheese each.

7. Bake in a preheated 350 degree oven for 15 minutes to melt the cheese.

Serve warm, with 1 potato and 1 pepper per person. **Serves 6**

Caigua Relleno (Trujillo)

STUFFED PERUVIAN GREEN GOURD

*This most popular and typical vegetable is nothing more than
a hollow shell whose destiny is to be filled. I have not been successful
in finding the botanical name for this green, odd-shaped, slightly
flattened green gourd. It has a neutral flavor.*

THE STUFFING

½   cup bread crumbs, moistened with
      3 tablespoons water

I   tablespoon corn oil

I   clove garlic, chopped

I   small onion, chopped (⅓ cup)

I   pound ground beef

I   teaspoon dried oregano

I   tablespoon chopped parsley

¼   teaspoon pepper

I   teaspoon salt, or to taste

¼   cup pitted black olives, halved

I   tablespoon raisins

2   hard-boiled eggs, peeled and quartered

8   *caigua*, tops cut off and inner seeds
      removed (see Note)

1. Prepare the stuffing: Process the moistened bread crumbs in a food
processor for ½ minute.

2. Heat the oil in a skillet. Add the garlic and onion and stir-fry over
low heat for 1 minute. Add the beef and fry it for 1 minute. Add all
the remaining ingredients, except the eggs and *caigua*. Fry the stuffing
for 3 minutes more, then fold in the egg quarters. Set the stuffing
aside and cool.

3. Stuff each *caigua* loosely with stuffing. Transfer into a saucepan
with ½ inch of water and 1 teaspoon salt. Cover the pan and simmer

over low heat for about 15 minutes. This is just enough to cook the *caigua* shells and heat the stuffing through.

Serve warm with rice and salads. **Serves 8**

Note: Since *caigua* is not available, to my knowledge, my teacher suggested that red or green peppers be used as a substitute. The cooking time should be extended by 10 minutes if using the bell peppers.

Puchero (Cuzco)

MEATS AT CARNIVAL

The Carnival celebration in February in Cuzco is a nonreligious fiesta of meat. The root of the word "carnival" is the Spanish word carne, *which means meat. It is a time of eating and street gaiety and lasts from three days to a week. Puchero is served at this time.*

I	**pound boneless beef steak or leg of lamb, cut into 6 pieces**
4	**cups (I quart) water**
I	**teaspoon dried oregano**
4	**whole allspice**
I	**teaspoon salt**
I	**pound yuca (see Glossary), peeled and cut into 6 equal pieces**
I	**pound potato, peeled and cut into 6 equal pieces**
2	**ears of corn, cut into 6 pieces, each 2 inches long**
½	**cup cooked chick peas**
½	**cup rice, well rinsed and cooked**
6	**pieces of cabbage (about 1½ pounds)**
6	**small whole peaches or pears**
3	**slices bacon, fried crisp and drained on paper towels**

1. In a pot cook the meat in the water with the oregano, allspice, and salt over moderate heat, covered, until tender, about 40 minutes. Remove the meat. Remove and reserve ½ cup of the broth.

2. Add the yuca, potato, and corn to the broth in the pot and cook over moderate heat until soft but not mushy. Remove and divide into separate mounds.

3. Cook the peaches in boiling water for 10 minutes. Drain.

4. Puchero is served in a ritualistic arrangement with all the ingredients allotted a place on the serving platter. The arrangement is as follows: The meat is placed in the center of the platter. Moving clockwise around the perimeter, the corn is placed on the 3 o'clock spot; the yuca and the potatoes at the 5 o'clock position; the peaches (or pears) a little farther around, on the 7 o'clock spot. The cabbage chunks should be placed at the top of the platter. The rice and chick peas, mixed together, cover the meat. The reserved ½ cut warm broth is then poured over all to keep the ingredients moist.

Serve warm. **Serves 6**

Cau-Cau, also called Mondongo (Chincha)
BEEF TRIPE STEW

It is difficult to explain why tripe has so many aficionados.
It is tough and chewy and requires considerable cooking. One buys it clean,
white, then proceeds from there. The idea is to surround the small cubes of
semi-cooked tripe with flavor, color, and the additional texture of potatoes.
That is what happens here. I do like tripe!

3	pounds white beef tripe
3	tablespoons corn oil
2	cloves garlic, ground to a paste with 2 tablespoons water
2	medium onions, chopped (1 cup)
½	teaspoon turmeric
1	teaspoon salt, or to taste
⅛	teaspoon pepper
⅛	teaspoon cumin
6	potatoes (2 pounds), peeled and cut into ½-inch cubes
1	cup water
½	cup fresh or frozen green peas
½	cup cubed carrot (¼ inch)
6	sprigs fresh cilantro, chopped
4	sprigs fresh mint, leaves only, chopped

1. Cover the tripe with water, bring a boil, and simmer, covered, over low heat for ½ hour, until tender. Drain, cool, and cut into ½-inch cubes.

2. Heat the oil in a pan, add the garlic paste, onions, turmeric, salt, pepper, and cumin and stir-fry over low heat for 2 minutes.

3. Now add the cubed tripe, potatoes, water, peas, and carrot and simmer over low heat for 20 minutes. Stir in the cilantro and mint and remove the pan from the heat. The stew will have only a small amount of sauce.

Serve warm, with white rice. **Serves 6 to 8**

Patito con Mani (Iquitos)

COW'S FEET IN PEANUT SAUCE

A number of cultures prepare cow's feet, the food of the poor.
The English, for example, enjoy cow's foot jelly, a cold gelatinous appetizer.
This is my first encounter with cow's feet prepared in a peanut sauce,
an imaginative idea. The dish can be seen on restaurant menus around the
country. Try it, you will like it. Cow's feet are also available at a good
meat market, where they can be cut to order.

2	pounds cow's feet and attached meat
8	cups (2 quarts) water
¼	cup corn oil
I	large onion, chopped (I cup)
2	cloves garlic, crushed
I	cup chopped tomato
I	teaspoon salt
¼	teaspoon pepper
¼	teaspoon cumin
½	teaspoon turmeric
I	pound potato, peeled and cut into ½-inch pieces
¾	cup dry roasted peanuts, coarsely ground

1. Have the butcher cut the cow's feet through the bone into round 1-inch slices with the meat attached. Bring the water to a boil, add the feet, and cook, covered, until tender, about 1 hour. (A pressure cooker is ideal for this.) Drain, and reserve 4 cups broth.

2. Heat the oil in a skillet. Add the onion and garlic and stir-fry over low heat for 2 minutes. Add the tomato, salt, pepper, cumin, and turmeric and stir-fry for 3 minutes. Add the cooked cow's feet and meat.

3. Now add the reserved broth, the potato, and ground peanuts. Combine well and cook for ½ hour.

Serve hot, with rice. **Serves 10**

Anticuchos (Trujillo)

BARBECUED SPICY BEEF HEARTS ON A SKEWER

*Peruvians dote on the anticuchos of beef heart, chicken gizzards,
beef liver, and the delectable tidbits of cow udders. This list is not terribly
enticing, but one should ignore the semantics and dig in. (For more
details, see the Note at the end of this recipe.)*

*After dark, the anticucho snack shops are thronged with
people chewing enthusiastically on the vividly seasoned cubes of mostly
beef heart that they wash down with beer or soft drinks as the aroma
of the barbecue pit swirls around them.*

*Anticuchos are the typical food of the Negro community who came as
slaves to Peru in the middle of the Nineteenth Century.*

6	pounds beef heart
I	tablespoon *achiote* granules (see Glossary), dissolved in 3 tablespoons hot corn oil
2	teaspoons salt
2	teaspoons cumin
2	teaspoons pepper
5	cloves garlic, ground fine
I	to 2 tablespoons chopped and seeded fresh *aji amarillo* (yellow Peruvian chili, see Glossary), ground to a paste with ½ cup water
I	cup distilled white vinegar
	Bamboo skewers, each 12 inches long and ¼ inch wide

1. Cut the beef hearts into quarters. Trim and discard the interior
veins and membranes, etc., leaving a shell of about ½ inch thick. Rinse
well in cold water. Cut into rectangular pieces, 1½ inches long by 2
inches wide.

2. In a large bowl combine the *achiote* oil, salt, cumin, pepper, garlic,
aji paste, and vinegar. Add the heart cubes, mix well, and marinate

preferably overnight; if not, then a minimum of 4 hours to absorb the array of flavors. Remove the cubes and reserve the marinade.

3. Push 4 or 5 seasoned cubes close together onto each skewer and press flat. Grill over charcoal, turning now and then, for about 5 minutes, brushing the skewers lightly with the reserved marinade.

Serve hot, as an evening snack food, with cooked 2-inch cubes of white potato pierced on the tip of each skewer. Slices of grilled cooked sweet potato are also served on the side. Occasionally, 2-inch wide rounds of *choclo* (white corn on the cob) are served, too. **Serves 4 to 6**

Note: Chicken gizzards are prepared the same way. Each lobe of the gizzard is sliced almost all the way through but still attached. Marinate and grill as directed above.

The cow udder is cut into strips, and first cooked in 4 cups water with 2 tablespoons salt for about 20 minutes, or until soft. Then it is marinated as the hearts are. The strips are then grilled whole but not on skewers, cut into cubes, and served. Beef liver is treated the same way as the udder is—that is to say, marinated, barbecued, cubed, and served.

Lengua de Res Atomatada (Cuzco)
BEEF TONGUE IN TOMATO SAUCE

Tongue is either going out of style in New York or is difficult to obtain. Yet people enjoy its flavor and texture; the Peruvians do. This Cuzco family-style recipe includes spaghetti and is a splendid one-dish meal.

THE TONGUE

8   cups (2 quarts) water
3   pounds beef or veal tongues, well rinsed
1   tablespoon salt

THE SAUCE

6	cloves garlic
½	teaspoon cumin
1	teaspoon dried oregano
2	tablespoons corn oil
6	cups peeled, chopped fresh tomatoes, or canned chopped
1	pound carrot, sliced and cooked until soft
1	pound onion, chopped
½	teaspoon sugar

THE SPAGHETTI

2	pounds thin spaghetti (#8 size), broken in half
1	teaspoon corn oil
1	teaspoon salt

1. Prepare the tongue: Bring the water to a boil in a large pan, add the tongues and salt and cook, covered, over low heat for 45 minutes, or until the tongue is tender. (See Note.) Remove the tongues, cool somewhat, and peel off the tough skin. Reserve 2 cups of the broth. Cut the tongues into ¼-inch-thick slices. Set aside.

2. Prepare the sauce: In a food processor process the garlic, cumin, and oregano until smooth. Heat the oil in a skillet and stir-fry the mixture over low heat for 2 minutes. Set aside.

3. In a food processor, purée the tomatoes to a smooth consistency. Push the purée through a metal sieve to remove the seeds. Remove. Process the carrot slices until smooth. Remove. Process the raw onions until smooth.

4. Combine the puréed tomatoes, carrot, and onion and the reserved tongue broth in a pan and simmer, covered, over low heat for ½ hour. Mix in the sugar. Add the tongue slices.

5. Prepare the spaghetti: While the tongue cooks, cook the spaghetti in water with the oil and salt for about 10 minutes (or less if you prefer it *al dente*). Drain.

6. Add to the pasta the sauce and tongue slices. Bring the mixture to a simmer and cook for 5 minutes. Adjust the salt and oregano if you wish.

Serve hot. **Serves 10**

Note: The tongues must be cooked until soft in the conventional manner. Pressure cookers are useful tools in the kitchens in Cuzco, and I recommend that they be used for this purpose. Cook the tongues for about 45 minutes. I do so myself in New York.

Chicarrónes de Chancho de Saylla (Cuzco)

CRISP PORK CUBES FROM SAYLLA

About a forty-five-minute drive from Cuzco, one enters the town of Saylla, situated in a beautiful narrow green valley. Hills surround the town on the east and west and lush green grass is everywhere. Cows and pigs graze up to their knees in the green and a brook runs through the valley with crystal clear water.

Coming in or going out of the town are the Quechua Indian ladies with their white stovepipe hats. They line the road, frying and selling these hot chicharrónes *and potatoes. That is all there is.*

4	pounds fresh pork from ribs and leg, including bones
1	tablespoon salt
2	cloves garlic, chopped
2	teaspoons cumin
1	cup water
3	pounds potatoes, peeled and cut into ½-inch-thick rounds

1. Cut the pork through the bones into 4-inch pieces. They may shrink considerably when cooked.

2. Put the pork, salt, garlic, cumin, and water in a large skillet and cover. Cook over moderate heat about ½ hour. When the meat is cooked, remove and set aside. Pour off all but a thin coating of the fat.

3. Add the potatoes to the skillet. Add the cooked pork and fry over high heat 15 to 20 minutes, turning the mixture, until the potatoes are crisp.

Serve warm, 3 or 4 pieces per person, accompanied by the crispy potatoes and a side dish of red onion salad and chopped mint leaves mixed with lime juice to taste. **Serves 8**

Adobo de Chancho (Puno)

PORK IN A SPICY SAUCE WITH POTATOES

Puno is high, about 12,000 feet, with a cold that penetrates after the sun descends. It is on the shores of Lake Titicaca, which was at a very low ebb during my visit. Off in the distance was Bolivia, an unknown culinary quantity.

It was in the public market where the home-cooking stalls were preparing regional foods for lunch, the foods of a high, cold climate, that I made a deal with a cook to prepare this Adobo together. "Chancho," the colloquial word for pork, is used all over Peru but is to me of unknown etymology.

2	tablespoons corn oil
5	cloves garlic, ground to a paste with 2 tablespoons water
I	large onion, coarsely chopped (I cup)
2	teaspoons finely chopped seeded fresh *aji amarillo* (yellow Peruvian chili, see Glossary), or I teaspoon dried yellow *aji* chili powder
4	pounds pork roast, with or without bone, cut into 8 pieces
I	teaspoon cumin
½	teaspoon paprika
I	teaspoon salt, or to taste
¼	teaspoon turmeric
6	cups water
8	cubes (I inch) peeled potatoes (about I pound)
¼	cup dry plain bread crumbs
I	pound yuca (see Glossary), peeled, cut into large thumb-sized pieces, and cooked

1. Heat the oil in a large pan. Add the garlic paste, onion, and *aji* and stir-fry over low heat for 2 minutes. Add the pork and stir-fry for 5 minutes. Add the cumin, paprika, salt, and turmeric and mix well.

2. Add the water and bring to a boil. Cover the pan and simmer 1 hour, or until the meat is tender but still firm.

3. Add the cubed potatoes and cook 15 minutes more, or until soft. Adjust the salt.

4. Lastly, add the bread crumbs to thicken the sauce. Simmer 3 minutes.

Serve hot, with the yuca as a side dish. **Serves 8**

Chancho con Salsa Tamarindo (Chinese)

BONELESS PORK IN TAMARIND SAUCE

Pork is a popular meat throughout Peru and is a natural with tamarind sauce.

1	**pound boneless pork, cut into 3 pieces**
4	**cups (1 quart) water**
1	**clove garlic, chopped**
1	**teaspoon chopped ginger**
2	**tablespoons corn oil**
2	**cups Tamarind Sauce with Pineapple (see 212), warmed**

1. In a large saucepan cook the pork in the water with the garlic and ginger over moderate heat for 45 minutes, or until tender. Drain, cool slightly, and cut into thin slices.

2. Heat the oil in a skillet and brown the slices rapidly over high heat for ½ minute. Add the slices to the warm tamarind sauce.

Serve immediately, with white rice and various salads. **Serves 6**

Chancho con Tamarindo (Iquitos)

PORK IN TAMARIND SAUCE AMAZON STYLE

*The influence is Peruvian-Chinese in this dish, which I had
in a Chifa restaurant in Iquitos. Peruvians throng to the Chifa restaurants
wherever they are found, which is everywhere. The food is always good
and in some places superb, as I discovered in Lima, too.*

2	tablespoons corn oil
2	cloves garlic, chopped
1	medium onion, chopped (½ cup)
2	pounds boneless pork, cut into 1½-inch strips
1	cup shredded cabbage
⅓	cup julienne sliced carrot
¼	cup tamarind paste, dissolved in ½ cup water and strained
1	teaspoon sugar, or more to taste
1	teaspoon salt
¼	teaspoon pepper
1	teaspoon cornstarch, dissolved in 1/4 cup water

1. Heat the oil in a wok or skillet. Add the garlic and onion and stir-fry over moderate heat for 2 minutes. Add the pork and fry, stirring, for 5 minutes to brown. Now add the cabbage and carrot and fry another minute to coat.

2. Add the tamarind liquid, sugar, salt, and pepper and stir-fry for 3 minutes. Stir in the cornstarch mixture and cook, stirring, for 2 minutes, or until lightly thickened.

Serve warm, with rice. **Serves 6 or 7**

Adobo de Chancho (Iquitos)

BONELESS PORK IN VINEGAR SAUCE

This is criollo *food, which implies a certain age to the recipe.
Tender pork cubes are flavored with domestic wine vinegar from Ica,
the wine-growing region of Peru.*

I	tablespoon corn oil
I	medium onion, chopped (½ cup)
2	cloves garlic, chopped
½	teaspoon turmeric
3	pounds boneless pork, cut into 3-inch pieces
2	tablespoons red wine vinegar
I	teaspoon salt, or to taste
¼	teaspoon pepper
4	cups (I quart) water
¼	cup plain dry bread crumbs, moistened with ⅓ cup water
2	eggs, beaten

1. Heat the oil in a large pan. Add the onion, garlic, and turmeric and stir-fry over low heat for 3 minutes. Add the pork, vinegar, and salt and stir-fry for 5 minutes as the color of the meat changes.

2. Add the water, bring to a boil, cover the pan, and cook for about 40 minutes to tenderize the meat. Stir in the moist bread crumbs and stir briskly to combine and prevent sticking.

3. Stir in the eggs and cook 5 minutes. Adjust the salt if necessary.

Serve warm, with rice. **Serves 6 to 8**

Adobo de Chancho (Arequipa)

PORK IN WINE

Peruvians often assign certain dishes to particular days. According to my teacher, this Adobo is cooked on Sundays for breakfast. Peru has a well-established wine industry, so there is always a source of wine and red wine vinegar.

3	pounds pork chops with bone, cut into 8 portions
2	cups dry red wine
¼	cup red wine vinegar
1	to 2 tablespoons finely chopped seeded fresh *aji amarillo* (yellow Peruvian chili, see Glossary), or 1 teaspoon dried yellow *aji* powder, or to taste
1	teaspoon salt, or to taste
1	teaspoon cumin
1	teaspoon dried oregano
4	whole allspice
8	cloves garlic, sliced
5	sprigs parsley, chopped
2	medium onions, quartered (1 cup)

1. Put the pork, wine, vinegar, *aji*, salt, cumin, oregano, and allspice into a large bowl.

2. In a food processor process the garlic and parsley into a paste with 1/4 cup water. Stir the paste into the pork mixture. Mix well and marinade the pork overnight in the refrigerator.

3. The next day, transfer the pork mixture to a saucepan. Bring to a boil over low heat and cook until the meat is tender, about ½ hour. Add the onions and simmer for 15 minutes. If the Adobo seems too dry, add ½ cup of water and cook to render only a small amount of sauce.

Serve hot, with bread. **Serves 6 to 8**

Carapulcra (Callao)

PORK AND FREEZE-DRIED POTATOES

*One of the extraordinary inventions of the Inca in the vast
cold altiplano of Peru was their method of guaranteeing a source of food for
the winter. They froze potatoes in the natural temperatures, then reconstituted
them in the kitchen during the nongrowing season. Carapulcra is a tasty
and filling way to use the freeze-dried potatoes, called* papa seca. *Here
they are combined with pork to make a substantial dish.*

2	cups *papa seca* (see Glossary)
3	tablespoons corn oil
2	pounds boneless pork, cut into 2-inch cubes
2	medium onions, chopped (1 cup)
5	cloves garlic, chopped in a food processor
1	teaspoon dried yellow *aji* chili powder (see Glossary)
⅛	teaspoon cumin
2	teaspoons salt, or to taste
	A 1-inch cinnamon stick
1	whole clove
3	cups water
½	cup dry roasted peanuts, ground but still with some texture
2	tablespoons dry white wine (optional)
¼	teaspoon dried oregano
1	pound yuca (see Glossary), peeled, cut into large thumb-sized pieces, and cooked, for serving

1. Toast the *papa seca* in a dry skillet over low heat for about 5 minutes, stirring continuously to prevent burning. Transfer to a sieve and rinse in cold water. Drain. Put the potatoes in a bowl, cover with water, and soak overnight. Drain, then rise in cold water. The potatoes will swell somewhat and are now ready to use.

2. Heat the oil in a skillet or pan. Add the pork and stir-fry it over moderate heat for 3 minutes. Add the onions, garlic, *aji* powder, cumin,

cinnamon stick, salt, clove, and fry for 5 minutes.

3. Add the potatoes and water. Cook, covered, over low heat for 20 minutes as the liquid reduces by half.

4. Now add the peanuts, wine (if used), and oregano and simmer for another 5 minutes, stirring well to combine.

Serve hot, with the yuca arranged around the perimeter of the serving platter.

Serve, with rice and Salsa Criolla (page 138). **Serves 8**

Pierna de Chancho (Cuzco)

ROAST LEG OF PORK MOUNTAIN STYLE

A family-style roast for special occasions. Meat is money, which is scarce in the Andean hills of Cuzco.

4	**pounds fresh pork leg**
3	**tablespoons fresh lime juice**
½	**cup beer**
4	**medium onions, quartered (3 cups)**
3	**teaspoons paprika**
2	**teaspoons cumin**
6	**cloves garlic, ground to a paste with 3 tablespoons water**
1	**tablespoon finely chopped seeded fresh *aji amarillo* (yellow Peruvian chili, see Glossary) or 2 teaspoons dried yellow *aji* chili powder**
1	**teaspoon salt, or to taste**
2	**teaspoons corn oil**
¾	**cup water**

1. Rub the pork all over with the lime juice and beer.

2. In a bowl mix together the onions, paprika, cumin, garlic paste, *aji*, salt, and oil. Make about 8 slits in the pork, each 1-inch deep, and fill with the seasoned spice mixture. (What remains can be put in the roasting pan.) Cover well and marinate in the refrigerator for 24 hours.

3. Put the pork in a roasting pan, add the water to the bottom of the pan, and roast the leg in a preheated 325 degree oven for 2 hours (or more) to insure the meat is cooked through. The top of the pork will become crisp.

Serve warm, with bread or tamales. **Serves 8**

Fricase de Chancho (Puno)
FRICASSEE OF PORK

In Puno pork is popular, and as one of the cooks at the public market there told me, "It keeps us warm at this altitude," which is about 12,000 feet.

2	teaspoons cumin
2	to 3 teaspoons dried yellow *aji* chili powder, to taste (see Glossary)
¼	teaspoon pepper
¼	teaspoon turmeric
5	cloves garlic, sliced
16	cups (4 quarts) water
5	pounds pork, shoulder or back, including bone, cut through bone into 8 pieces
½	cup plain dry bread crumbs
2	teaspoons salt, or to taste
1	tablespoon red wine vinegar

1. In a processor grind together the cumin, *aji* powder, pepper, turmeric, and garlic. Set aside.

2. Bring the water to a boil in a large pan. Add the pork and ground seasonings and cook over moderate heat for 15 minutes. Add the bread crumbs and salt and mix well. Cook, covered, for 1½ hours (or more), until the meat is soft. Stir in the wine vinegar. The fricassee will develop a thick sauce, but if it is too thick, add a small amount of boiling water.

Serve hot, with white rice and white or yellow corn kernels. It can also be served, if preferred, with boiled potatoes. **Serves 8**

Frito de Chancho (Chiclayo)

PORK FRY WITH VEGETABLES

*The public market of Chiclayo is untidy; it pours out into the
street and is open to the air. On a second level, the comedors, eating houses,
are lined up one after another with a few tables and chairs. At each,
there is a small menu of the day, freshly cooked and very inexpensive. This
pork fry was $1.20 for a generous portion that included rice and beans.
The owner, a chunky lady, exhorted those who passed in the narrow lane of
the virtues of her cooking from the restaurant's very entrance.*

¼	cup corn oil
5	cloves garlic, chopped
2	pounds boneless pork, cut into 3-inch pieces
1	teaspoon salt, or to taste
½	teaspoon pepper
½	teaspoon cumin
⅓	cup distilled white vinegar
1	to 1½ cups water
2	pounds sweet potatoes, cut into 3-inch-long by ½-inch-thick pieces and cooked, for serving
2	pounds yuca (see Glossary), peeled, cut into long pieces, each ½-inch thick, and cooked, for serving

1. Heat the oil in a pan. Add the garlic, pork, salt, pepper, and cumin and stir-fry over low heat for about 15 minutes.

2. Add the vinegar and 1 cup water. Bring to a boil, cover the pan, and simmer until almost all the liquid has evaporated and the meat is tender, about 25 minutes. Should the pork still be too firm, add another ½ cup water and continue to simmer until tender.

Serve warm, with the sweet potatoes and yuca on the side of the platter and the pork in the center. A side dish of Zarza Red Onion Condiment, page 204, is ubiquitous. **Serves 6**

Chorizo (Iquitos)
PORK SAUSAGE AMAZON STYLE

One sees these homemade sausage hanging up for sale at the public markets. They are simply made and best eaten fresh.

2	**pounds boneless pork, cubed**
1	**pound bacon, cubed**
⅛	**teaspoon ground nutmeg**
1	**teaspoon salt**
¼	**teaspoon cumin**

1. Grind all the ingredients together in a food processor until chopped but not too fine. There should be some texture.

2. Stuff the mixture into sausage casing, available at most Italian meat markets. Cut into 4-inch-long pieces when you are ready to cook the sausages.

The best method is to barbecue the sausages over charcoal until crisp. If not, fry them without oil in a skillet until crisp. Discard all the fat. **Makes 10 sausages**

Sancochado Criollo (All Peru)

MEAT AND VEGETABLE BOILED DINNER

This is a grand creole family and friend production where the quantity, quality, and variety of three meats and an assortment of vegetables producing a richly flavored consommé are served with an excess of generosity. Peruvians like to eat!

The quantities noted below can easily serve 15 people, but can just as easily be reduced for 10 or even 5 without eliminating any of the variety. A little judicious studying of the recipe will provide all the information needed to do so.

6	quarts water
1	tablespoon salt, or to taste
	A 5-pound whole hen (do not use young chicken)
4	pounds short ribs of beef, excess fat trimmed
2	pounds boneless pork, in 1 piece
10	small whole carrots
	Whole ripe small peaches, 6 per person, do not peel
1	small whole bunch celery, trimmed
2	whole green Savoy cabbage heads (about 4 pounds)
4	pounds *Zapallo* (see Glossary) or butternut squash, peeled
5	ears of corn
10	small whole potatoes (about 2 pounds), peeled
5	whole sweet potatoes (2 pounds), peeled
5	whole green plantains, peeled

1. Bring the water and salt to a boil in a large pot. Add the hen and cook, covered, over moderate heat for 15 minutes. Add the short ribs and cook for 15 minutes; add the pork and simmer the 3 meats until almost tender but still quite firm, about ½ hour.

2. Now add the vegetables and fruit; the carrots first, then the peaches, celery, cabbage, squash, and potatoes and cook until soft, about 15 to 20 minutes. Lastly, add the corn and cook for 5 minutes. One must be prepared for the variability in the firmness of the meats

and vegetables; some might require a few minutes here or there of additional cooking.

3. Cook the sweet potatoes and plantains separately from the meats and vegetables. When soft, remove from the water and set aside.

Do not overcook the meats or vegetables. There should be a tender firmness to the meats and a light crunch to the vegetables, except the potatoes, plantains, and squash, which should be soft. It may be necessary to add more water during the cooking process if the liquid evaporates too quickly.

4. Serve in the following traditional manner: The meat is sliced into standard pieces; the hen carved from the bone. Place the meats in separate piles in the center of a large serving platter. Arrange the cooked vegetables in aesthetic combinations around the perimeter of the platter as follows:

Cut the carrots into generous diagonal slices. The celery, divided into stalks, should be halved. Each head of cabbage should be cut into 4 equal pieces, central core removed. Cut each ear of corn into 4 or 5 piece rounds. Serve the white potatoes whole. The sweet potatoes and plantains should be cut into generous slices.

5. Adjust the salt in the cooking broth and bring the broth to a boil. Serve the consommé throughout the meal in standard tea cups or mugs since it is eaten with the other foods.

6. As a contrast to the broth, meat, and vegetables, it is customary to serve three different salsas.

Salsa Criolla

ONION AND LIME JUICE SIDE DISH

2   **cups thinly sliced red onions**

1   **teaspoon chopped, seeded fresh *aji amarillo* (yellow Peruvian chili, see Glossary) or ½ teaspoon of dried yellow *aji* chili**

3	to 4 tablespoons fresh lime juice, or more to taste
I	teaspoon salt
I	tablespoon chopped fresh cilantro leaves

Mix all the ingredients together at serving time. **Makes 2 cups**

Salsa con Queso
WHITE CHEESE SAUCE

I	cup crumbled *queso fresco* (see Glossary) or Feta cheese
I	teaspoon olive oil
2	tablespoons evaporated or fresh milk
½	teaspoon chopped seeded fresh *aji amarillo* (see above)
I	to 2 tablespoons *huacatay* (see Glossary)

Process all the ingredients in a blender until fairly smooth. Adjust the amount of *huacatay* to your taste. Serve at room temperature. **Makes 1¼ cups**

Salta Piquante con Tomate
SPICY SAUCE

I	cup chopped ripe tomato
I	to 2 teaspoons chopped seeded fresh *aji amarillo* (see above)
2	cloves garlic, chopped fine
2	tablespoons chopped red onion
I	tablespoon chopped fresh cilantro

Process all the ingredients together in a food processor to create a smooth sauce. Serve at room temperature. **Makes 1 cup**

Sopa Seca (Chincha)

SPAGHETTI WITH TWO MEATS

Beef, pork, and the ubiquitous and melting potato enrich spaghetti here. The Italians have left their mark on the cooking of the Chincha Negroes, who have, in turn, added their own style of seasonings in this cross-cultural production.

1	tablespoon corn oil
2	cloves garlic, ground to a paste with 2 tablespoons water
1	medium onion, chopped (½ cup)
⅛	teaspoon pepper
⅛	teaspoon ground cumin
1	teaspoon salt, or to taste
½	cup chopped ripe tomato
1	pound boneless beef, cut into 1-inch cubes
1	pound boneless pork, cut into 1-inch cubes
3	small potatoes, peeled and cut into ½-inch dice
2½	cups water
1	pound spaghetti (#8 size), broken in half
6	sprigs fresh cilantro, chopped

1. Heat the oil in a pan. Add the garlic, onion, pepper, cumin, salt, and tomato and stir-fry for 2 minutes. Add the 2 meats and potatoes and fry over low heat for 5 minutes.

2. Add 1 cup of the water, cover the pan, and cook until the meats are almost tender, about 45 minutes.

3. Add the spaghetti to the pan with the remaining 1½ cups water and bring to a boil. Cook over low heat for 15 minutes until *al dente*. Stir in the cilantro. The *sopa seca* should be moist, the meat tender, but there should be very little sauce.

Serve warm. **Serves 8 to 10**

Sopa de Frijol (Chincha)

BEAN AND TWO-MEAT STEW

Yellow beans are typically Peruvian and the bean of choice there.
They are light yellow in color, with rounded ends, and are medium in size.
They can be found in Peruvian grocery stores in the United States.

1	pound (2 cups) dried yellow beans, soaked overnight in water to cover, then drained
4	cups (1 quart) water
1	pound boneless beef chuck, cut into 1-inch cubes
1	pound boneless pork, cut into 1-inch cubes
2	ounces *chalona* (dried salted beef, optional)
2	teaspoons corn oil
1	clove garlic, chopped
1	small onion, chopped (¼ cup)
1	teaspoon salt
⅛	teaspoon pepper
½	pound *Zapallo* (see Glossary) or butternut squash, peeled and cut into ½-inch cubes
1	pound potatoes (2 or 3), peeled and cut into ½-inch cubes
1	cup ziti or similar tubular pasta

1. Cook the beans in the water, covered, over low heat until only half cooked, about ½ hour. Add the beef, pork, and salt beef (if used).

2. Meanwhile, heat the oil in a skillet. Add the garlic, onion, salt, and pepper and stir-fry over low heat for 3 minutes. Add to the bean mixture.

3. Add the squash, potatoes, and pasta and cook over low-to-moderate heat for 15 minutes, enough to soften all the ingredients. If still too firm, cook 10 minutes longer. This is a thick stew.

Serve hot. **Serves 6 to 8**

Arroz Chaufa Mixto (Lima)

FRIED RICE WITH ASSORTED MEATS

Although there is a similarity between classic Chinese cooking and the cooking that is produced in the Chifa restaurants in Lima, there are differences that identify the cross-cultural mixture, give or take a century or two.

3	tablespoons corn oil
4	eggs, beaten
4	cups cooked rice, cold
¼	teaspoon chopped ginger
½	cup roasted or boiled pork, cut into ½-inch cubes
½	cup cooked chicken, cut into ½-inch cubes
½	cup cooked peeled medium shrimp
½	cup thinly sliced scallions
¼	teaspoon sesame oil
1	tablespoon light soy sauce
¼	teaspoon salt

THE SPINACH

1	tablespoon corn oil
1	clove garlic, crushed
1	thick slice ginger, crushed
	Salt to taste
½	pound fresh spinach leaves, well rinsed

1. Heat the oil in a wok. Add the beaten eggs and scramble them over moderate heat. Immediately add the rice, pork, chicken, shrimp, and scallions and continue to stir-fry everything together until heated through.

2. Add the sesame oil, soy sauce, and salt and toss well. Remove and keep warm. Serve warm. **Serves 6**

3. Make the spinach: Heat the oil in a wok or skillet. Add the garlic, ginger, and salt and stir-fry over high heat for 2 minutes. Add the spinach and stir-fry 2 minutes more until just wilted. Serve as a side dish with the rice.

Seco de Cordero (Arequipa)

LAMB, DRY ROAST

This is a comida criolla, *that is to say, it is a colonial-type dish prepared by the new community in Peru, a culinary mixture of the indigenous Indians and the Spanish.* Criolla *food was prepared over a wood stove in clay pots, which gave it a certain cachet that is still appreciated. The* picanterias *of Arequipa and other towns still use wood fires to advertise their traditional methods.*

20	long sprigs fresh cilantro
3	cups water
3	tablespoons corn oil
3	cloves garlic, ground to a paste with 2 tablespoons water
2	medium onions, chopped (1 cup)
¼	teaspoon turmeric
4	pounds lamb ribs with bone, fat trimmed, cut into 8 pieces
2	pounds small potatoes (8), peeled
2	carrots, cut into small dice (1 cup)
½	cup fresh or frozen green peas
2	teaspoons salt, or to taste
¼	teaspoon pepper
6	whole allspice
1	teaspoon dried oregano

1. Trim off the stems of the cilantro sprigs, cut them up, and process them to a smooth paste with ¼ cup water.

2. Heat the oil in a pan. Add the garlic paste, onions, and turmeric and stir-fry over low heat for 2 minutes. Add the cilantro paste and lamb and stir-fry for 15 minutes to brown the meat.

3. Add the remaining 2¾ cups water and bring it to a boil. Add potatoes, carrots, peas, salt, pepper, allspice, and oregano, cover, and cook for ½ hour. Test the lamb and potatoes for doneness. If too firm, simmer until tender. Adjust salt. There should be some sauce (despite the English title of this recipe).

Serve hot, with white rice. **Serves 6 to 8**

Seco de Cabrito (Chincha)

LAMB STEW FROM CHINCHA

Actually a cabrito *is a young goat or kid, but since these are not always available and lamb has become the meat of choice, I am using lamb in both the title and stew. This Seco has a lot going for it, with the cilantro and Chicha de jora (or beer) sauce, both of which emphasize the flavor of the lamb.*

I	cup *chicha de jora* (see **Note**) or substitute 1 cup beer
I	teaspoon salt, or to taste
⅛	teaspoon pepper
¼	teaspoon ground cumin
4	cloves garlic, ground to a paste with 3 tablespoons water
2	pounds leg of lamb or ribs, cut into 3-inch pieces
¼	cup corn oil
2	medium onions, chopped (1 cup)
I	cup cilantro leaves, ground to a paste with ⅓ cup water

1. Combine the *chicha* or beer with the salt, pepper, cumin, and garlic paste. Add the lamb and marinate it for ½ hour.

2. Heat the oil in a pan. Add the onions and stir-fry them over low heat until they become golden. Add the lamb and marinade and stir-

fry for 5 minutes as the meat changes color. Add the cilantro paste and mix well. Cover the pan and cook over low heat for ½ hour, or until the lamb is tender. The sauce that accumulates will be green.

Serve warm, with yellow beans and white rice. **Serves 6 to 8**

Note: Chicha de jora is a fermented corn drink of pre-Inca origin and is still prepared today as a home brew. The corn is cooked, then fermented for 8 days before it is used as a social drink or as a flavoring agent in meat dishes. If you have Peruvian connections in the United States, you may be able to find it. If not, beer is a very acceptable substitute.

Seco de Cordero (Trujillo)

LAMB STEW WITH VEGETABLES

*These northern stews are variations of one another. Some
have assorted vegetables, as this one does; another has a wine sauce;
and some have fresh yellow* aji, *which is only semi-hot, especially
when the seeds have been removed.*

2	pounds lamb, shoulder or leg, with or without bone, cut into 3-inch pieces
1	teaspoon salt, or to taste
¼	teaspoon pepper
1	tablespoon red wine vinegar
¼	teaspoon dried oregano
¼	teaspoon cumin
3	tablespoons corn oil
2	to 3 tablespoons dried yellow *aji* chili powder (see Glossary)
¼	cup chopped onion
¼	teaspoon turmeric
1	sprig cilantro, chopped fine
½	cup fresh or frozen green peas
½	cup sliced carrot
1	pound potatoes, cut as for French fries
2	cups water

1. In a large bowl mix the lamb with the salt, pepper, vinegar, oregano, and cumin and let stand for 10 minutes.

2. In a large pan heat the oil. Add the *aji* powder, onion, turmeric, and cilantro and stir fry over low heat for 2 minutes. Add the lamb, peas, carrot, and potatoes. Mix to combine, cover, and cook for 3 minutes. Add the water, bring to a boil, cover, and cook for 45 minutes, or until the lamb is tender and the sauce thickened.

Serve warm, with rice. **Serves 6**

〜〜〜 OTHER MEATS 〜〜〜

Cabrito Chiclayano (Chiclayo)
PAN-ROASTED RIBS OF KID

Tender, young kid is cooked all over the western coast of Peru. This combination is in the style of Chiclayo, a city known for its good food.

2	pounds ribs of kid, cut into 8 equal parts (see **Note**)
½	cup cider vinegar
5	cloves garlic, ground to a paste with 2 tablespoons water
1	teaspoon salt, or to taste
¼	teaspoon pepper
½	teaspoon turmeric
3	tablespoons corn oil
10	sprigs fresh cilantro, sliced
2	fresh *aji amarillo* (yellow Peruvian chili, see Glossary), seeded and sliced, or 1 teaspoon dried yellow *aji* chili powder
¼	cup cubed peeled *Zapallo* (see Glossary) or butternut squash
¼	cup water
2	pounds yuca (see Glossary), peeled and cut into index-finger-sized pieces and cooked, for serving

1. Put the ribs in a large bowl and add the vinegar, garlic paste, salt, pepper, and turmeric. Stir well and marinate for a minimum of 1 hour.

2. Heat the oil in a large pan. Add the meat and marinade and stir-fry over low heat for 2 minutes to lightly brown the meat. Cover the pan and cook gently for 15 minutes.

3. Meanwhile, in a food processor grind the cilantro, *aji*, squash, and water to a smooth paste.

4. When the ribs have cooked for 15 minutes, add the cilantro mixture to the stew. Mix well and cook for 20 minutes more, or until the meat is tender. Should the liquid evaporate too quickly, add another ½ cup water. There should be very little sauce.

Serve warm, with the yuca; garnish the meat with ½ cup Zarza (page 201). **Serves 8**

Seco de Cabrito (Trujillo)
KID STEW WITH RED WINE

There are vineyards in Peru and wine to heighten the culinary offerings there. Here is a stew with only a little sauce from northern Peru, where the cooking differs substantially from that in the southern part. A kid is a very young goat. It is available in certain ethnic markets, particularly of the Caribbean.

The same recipe may be prepared with 2 pounds of hen—breast, thigh, leg, cut into 6 to 8 pieces. The cooking time is approximately the same.

2	pounds young kid, with or without bone, cut into 8 pieces
1	teaspoon salt
½	teaspoon dried oregano
½	cup red wine plus 1/4 teaspoon wine vinegar
3	tablespoons corn oil
2	teaspoons dried yellow *aji* chili powder (see Glossary)
1	pound onion (1 large), chopped
1	sprig cilantro, chopped

1. Rub the kid with the salt, oregano, and wine. Let stand 1 to 3 hours (longer is better).

2. Heat the oil in a medium pan. Add the onion and stir-fry over low heat for 2 minutes. Mix in the *aji* powder and stir-fry for 2 to 3 minutes.

3. Add the meat and marinade and cilantro and stir well. Cover the pan and cook over low heat for 45 minutes, or until the meat is tender. Should the stew require more time and, therefore, more liquid, add ½ cup hot water. Stir in the wine vinegar.

Serve warm, with rice, beans, and boiled yuca pieces. **Serves 6**

Seco de Cabrito (Lima)

YOUNG KID STEW

The word seco *indicates that there will be some but not very much sauce. A cabrito is a young goat (kid) and it is eaten exclusively in the northern part of Peru. In the southern part, it is lamb (cordero).*

Chicken pieces or shoulder lamb chops may be prepared in the same way as the kid. The cooking time will be the same.

- 1   **cup fresh cilantro leaves**
- ½   **teaspoon chopped seeded fresh *aji amarillo* (yellow Peruvian chili, see Glossary), or dried yellow *aji* chili powder**
- 2   **tablespoons corn oil**
- 2   **cloves garlic, chopped**
- ¼   **cup chopped onion**
- 4   **pounds young kid with bone (shank and ribs), cut through the bone into 3-inch pieces**
- 1¼   **cups water**
- 2   **teaspoons salt, or to taste**
- 2   **pounds yuca (see Glossary), peeled, cut into thumb-sized pieces, and cooked, for serving**

1. Blend the cilantro and *aji* powder with 3 tablespoons water in a food processor until smooth.

2. Heat the oil in a large pan. Add the garlic and onion and stir-fry over moderate heat for 2 minutes. Add the kid pieces and cilantro paste and continue to stir-fry for 10 minutes to brown the meat.

3. Add the water and salt, cover, and cook over low heat for about 40 minutes, or until the meat is tender. There will be only a little sauce.

Serve warm, with rice and the yuca. **Serves 6 to 8**

Chirimpico (Chiclayo)
TRIPE STEW OF YOUNG KID

One always hears about young kid (cabrito) and not goat, which is used for procreation rather than food. And the tripe of the kids is popular and prepared all over the country. Chirimpico, from the northern city of Chiclayo, is a regional dish that has intriguing ingredients in the Peruvian style. It is lusty in flavor. Cooked beef tripe may be used instead of kid tripe.

3	tablespoons corn oil
4	cloves garlic, chopped fine
¼	cup chopped onion
¼	cup chopped seeded tomato, fresh or canned
I	fresh yellow *aji amarillo* (yellow Peruvian chili, see Glossary), seeded and chopped
¼	fresh or frozen green peas
I	teaspoon salt, or to taste
¼	teaspoon pepper
¼	teaspoon cumin
¼	teaspoon turmeric
4	sprigs fresh cilantro, chopped
2	pounds potatoes, peeled and cut into ½-inch cubes
3	pounds cooked kid tripe, cut into ½-inch cubes
I½	cups water
½	teaspoon *pisco* (see Glossary, optional)

1. Heat the oil in a pan. Add the garlic, onion, tomato, *aji*, peas, salt, pepper, cumin, turmeric, and cilantro and stir-fry over low heat for 3 minutes. Add the potatoes and tripe and mix well.

2. Add the water and *pisco* (if used) and simmer over low heat for 20 minutes to soften the potatoes and integrate the sauce, which should thicken.

Serve, with white rice. **Serves 8**

Saltado de Alpaca (Puno)

ALPACA STEAK STIR-FRY

*Alpacas make up the largest number of camelidae in the rarefied
atmosphere of the Andes Mountains, along with the llamas. Alpaca is the
cheapest meat available to the people of Puno on Lake Titicaca; it is rich in
protein, almost fat free, and low in cholesterol.*

*This recipe leans on the Chinese for its inspiration; the technique of stir-frying
and the use of soy sauce of a very good quality, which is manufactured in
Peru. One hears the word* sillau *(pronounced see-yow), which is soy sauce,
mentioned all over the country, testimony to the influence that the Peruvian
Chinese have had in their Chifa restaurants.*

2	tablespoons corn oil
1½	pounds alpaca steak, cut into ½-inch cubes (see Note)
1	teaspoon salt, or to taste
¼	teaspoon pepper
¼	teaspoon cumin
3	cloves garlic, ground to a paste with 2 tablespoons water
1	teaspoon dried oregano
3	medium onions, cut into long, thin slices (1½ cups)
1	teaspoon finely chopped seeded fresh *aji amarillo* (yellow Peruvian chili, see Glossary) or 1 teaspoon dried yellow *aji* chili powder
2	teaspoons soy sauce
1	teaspoon red wine vinegar
1	cup sliced peeled ripe tomato
1½	pounds potatoes, peeled, cut, and cooked as French fries (see Step 2, page 28)
1	tablespoon chopped parsley

1. Heat the oil in a large skillet or wok. Add the alpaca steak, salt,
pepper, cumin, garlic, and oregano, and stir-fry a minute to coat over
moderate heat. Cover the skillet and fry for 3 minutes.

2. Add the onions, *aji*, soy sauce, and vinegar and stir well. Then add the tomato, mix it in quickly, and fold in the French fries. Garnish with the parsley.

Serve hot, with white rice. **Serves 6 to 8**

Note: There are specialty shops in New York City that deal in wild game of many types. They may have alpaca steak or be able to get it.

Guiso de Venado (Iquitos)

DEER STEAK IN RED SAUCE

The Amazon jungle reveals itself with an assortment of wild life that is edible and available. One morning for breakfast in the hotel I was served alligator chicharrónes *that tasted like veal; deer steaks like lamb, and a crisp fried caterpillar like peanuts. So what else is new?*

2	tablespoons corn oil
3	cloves garlic, crushed to a paste
¼	teaspoon pepper
¼	teaspoon cumin
3	pounds boneless deer steak cut into 3-inch pieces (see **Note**)
10	sprigs fresh cilantro, chopped
1	sweet red pepper, cut into 1-inch cubes (1 cup)
2	carrots, sliced thin (1 cup)
2½	cups water
1	teaspoon salt, or to taste

1. Heat the oil in a pan. Add the garlic, pepper, and cumin and stir-fry over low heat for 1 minute. Add the deer and stir-fry for 10 minutes.

2. In a food processor process together the cilantro, bell pepper, and carrots with ½ cup of the water to a smooth consistency. Add it to the deer mixture with the salt and remaining 2 cups water and bring to a boil. Cover and simmer over low heat for about 20 minutes, until the meat is tender. The sauce will be thick and red.

Serve warm, with rice. **Serves 8**

Note: In certain areas, like Vermont, where I grew up, deer meat will be available during the hunting season.

Cuy Frito (Trujillo)
CRISP FRIED GUINEA PIGS

It is quite possible in Peru that the cuy (guinea pig) was a prominent source of meat protein before the arrival of the Spanish in the Sixteenth Century with their pigs, cows, goats, sheep, chickens and ducks. Peruvians today wax enthusiastically about cuy, and many of them keep them in their houses or backyards as a permanent source of food. They are not everyday food, but are saved for special occasions. Those who will not eat them refer to these fur-covered mammals in uncomplimentary nonculinary terms which will not be repeated here. I tried Cuy Frito and liked it very much.

- 1   **cleaned cuy, about 2 pounds**
- ½   **teaspoon salt**
- ¼   **teaspoon pepper**
- ¼   **teaspoon cumin**
- 2   **cloves garlic, ground to a paste with 2 tablespoons water**
- 1   **cup corn oil**

THE POTATOES

- 2   **pounds medium potatoes, peeled and cut into ½-inch cubes**
- 2   **teaspoons finely chopped seeded *aji amarillo* (Peruvian chili, see Glossary) or 1 teaspoon dried yellow *aji* chili powder**
- 1   **teaspoon paprika for color**

1. Mix the *cuy* with the seasonings, including the garlic paste. Heat the oil in a wok or skillet. Fry the *cuy* over low heat for 15 minutes, until brown and crisp. Remove to paper towel to drain.

2. Meanwhile, prepare the potatoes: Cook all the ingredients together in water until the potatoes are soft, about 20 minutes. Drain.

To serve, arrange the potatoes on a serving platter and cover them with tender crisp fried *cuy*.

Serve warm. **Serves 4**

Guiso del Cuy (Trujillo)
GUINEA PIG STEW

Walking through public markets with an eye on the meat departments, one can find guinea pigs (cuy) ready for the pot. They are well cleaned and spread out in the characteristic butterfly presentation. They cost about $4.00 each.

1	cleaned cuy (guinea pig), about 2 pounds, cut into 4 equal parts
¼	teaspoon salt
¼	teaspoon pepper
1	teaspoon dried oregano
1	teaspoon cumin
1	teaspoon chopped cilantro
2	cloves garlic, ground to a paste with 2 tablespoons water
1	small onion, chopped (⅓ cup)
1	teaspoon paprika
1	tablespoon dried yellow *aji* chili powder (see Glossary)
3	tablespoons corn oil
1	cup water

1. Mix the *cuy* with all the ingredients, except the oil and water, and let stand 15 minutes.

2. Heat the oil in a pan. Add the *cuy* and marinade, and fry over low heat, browning it on both sides, for 5 minutes. Add the water, cover the pan, and simmer the stew for about 15 minutes, until the meat is tender.

Serve hot, with rice or plain boiled potatoes. **Serves 4**

Pepian de Conejo (Cuzco)
RABBIT STEW WITH PEANUTS

This is a classic dish of the mountain people, the Quechuas, of Cuzco. Wild rabbits are caught and served up in this inventive sauce of peanut, oregano, paprika, and garlic, among other things.

2	pounds rabbit, cut into 4 pieces
½	cup plain dry bread crumbs
½	cup corn oil
4	cloves garlic, crushed
I	medium onion, chopped
I	teaspoon paprika
I	teaspoon salt, or to taste
I	teaspoon dried oregano
⅛	teaspoon pepper
4	cups (I quart) water
8	small potatoes, about 1½ inches in diameter, peeled
⅓	cup dry roasted peanuts, ground fine

1. Dredge the rabbit pieces firmly in the bread crumbs.

2. Heat the oil in a skillet and fry the rabbit over low heat for 1 minute on each side. Remove and set aside.

3. Remove all but 1 tablespoon oil from the skillet. Add the garlic, onion, paprika, salt, oregano, and pepper and stir-fry for 2 minutes. Add the water and bring to a boil. Add the potatoes, rabbit, and ground peanuts and cook for about 20 minutes, or until the potatoes and rabbit are soft. Adjust the salt, if necessary.

Serve warm, with rice. **Serves 4**

Higado de Tortuga (Iquitos)
FRIED TURTLE LIVER

This is the Amazon and turtle from the river is available, although not conspicuously sold. It is illegal to kill land or river turtles but with a wink or a nod it becomes available. My favorite family restaurant in Iquitos kept me informed of the forbidden culinary fruit.

The liver was fried for just a short time and remarkably tender. It was the first and probably the last time I shall taste this unique dish.

½	**pound river turtle liver, cut into thin slices about ¼-inch thick**
1	**teaspoon salt**
⅛	**teaspoon cumin**
1	**tablespoon corn oil**

1. Rub the liver with the salt and cumin.

2. Heat the oil in a skillet and fry the liver lightly over low heat for about 2 minutes.

Serve immediately, while still warm, as an appetizer. **Serves 4**

Note: The open-air public market in Iquitos displayed a number of unconventional fish that looked like black prehistoric monsters, jungle fruit, as well as *suri de aguaje,* which is an edible caterpillar. There were buyers for everything.

dee dad de nueue anos

urue asu pare y al casique en esta

CHICKEN, DUCK, AND OTHER POULTRY

Peruvian cooking surprises. Poultry, the basis for so many dishes, competes with seafood as the primary source of protein. Cross-cultural recipes, derived from the creole community and then incorporating Italian ideas, Chinese technique, Japanese traditions, and the mores of the Negro community, all rely on chicken or hen. Many dishes call for hen, large and firm-fleshed, and to the Peruvians more desirable than younger smaller chicken. But it is duck that exerts its magic and prestige. Peruvians are duck-eaters. The city of Trujillo in the north has an area on the outskirts of the center known as "the duck circuit," where large outdoor restaurants specialize in the most popular recipe, duck with rice. And in the tropical city of Iquitos, on the Amazon River, you also find duck, jungle style. It is the large, meaty *pato*, male duck, that is preferred.

Turkey, pigeon, and an occasional wild duck, or aquatic bird, are of minor interest.

Aquadito de Pollo (Puno)

SOUPY CHICKEN WITH RICE

For chilly days when the sun glares brightly over Lake Titicaca (at an altitude of about 12,000 feet) and sometimes on frigid evenings, this soup warms the soul and spirit. For very little money, the comedors (eating kiosks) in the public market in Puno serve this substantial combination to hungry shoppers.

2	cups fresh cilantro leaves
6	cups water
2	tablespoons corn oil
3	cloves garlic, chopped fine
I	small onion, chopped (⅓ cup)
2	large sweet red peppers, seeded and chopped (2 cups)
½	cup chopped boneless chicken (½-inch pieces)
I	pound chicken gizzards, including the liver and heart (*menudencia*), trimmed, and the liver cut into lobes
I	pound potatoes, peeled, and cut into ¼-inch cubes
I	stalk celery heart, chopped
I	cup rice, well rinsed, soaked in water for 1/2 hour, and drained
½	cup fresh or frozen green peas
I	large carrot, cut into ¼-inch dice (I cup)
I	teaspoon salt, or to taste
¼	teaspoon pepper

1. In a food processor blend the cilantro to a smooth paste with ¼ cup water.

2. Heat 1 tablespoon of the oil in a skillet and stir-fry the cilantro paste over low heat for 2 minutes. Set aside.

3. Heat the remaining 1 tablespoon oil in the skillet, add the garlic, onion, red peppers, chicken, and *menudencia*, and stir-fry over low heat for 3 minutes.

4. In a large pot bring the remaining 5¾ cups water to a boil. Add the chicken and *menudencia* mixture, the cilantro paste, the potatoes, celery, rice, peas, carrot, salt, and pepper. Cover the pan and cook over low heat for 45 minutes, which should tenderize it all.

Serve hot. **Serves 8**

Pollo con Yuyo (Trujillo)

BONELESS CHICKEN BITS WITH CLOUD EARS

Heng Lung, just off the beautiful, if not grandiose, Plaza de Armas in Trujillo, was my first Chifa restaurant in Peru. These ubiquitous Chinese/Peruvian eateries often serve as an oasis in an unknown desert, where their good food is always available when all else fails. The origin of the cooking is Chinese and the flavors are recognizable, but have an off-beat slant that is original.

Yuyo are cloud ears—the small, thin, dried fungus used in traditional Chinese cooking. They provide texture rather than important flavor. Yuyo is also the word for the fresh seaweed that is gathered off the coastal waters of Peru for export, but which is included in some traditional dishes as well.

1	tablespoon corn oil
1	small clove garlic, chopped fine
½	cup yuyo (cloud ears), soaked in water 1 hour to soften, and drained
½	boneless skinless chicken breast, cut into little-finger-sized pieces
8	to 10 fresh snow peas
6	to 8-inch-square pieces sweet red pepper
¼	teaspoon sugar
1	teaspoon light soy sauce
½	cup chicken broth
1	teaspoon cornstarch, dissolved in 3 tablespoons water

1. Heat the oil in a wok and stir-fry the garlic over high heat for a few seconds. Add the cloud ears and chicken and stir-fry for 2 minutes.

2. Add the snow peas and red pepper and stir-fry another minute. Add the sugar, soy sauce, and broth and continue to stir-fry to combine. Last, pour in the cornstarch mixture, and stir until thickened to the desired consistency (about 1 minute).

Serve hot, with white rice. **Serves 2**

Milanesa de Pollo (Callao)

BREAST OF CHICKEN ITALIAN STYLE

Cross-cultural cooking is not new to Peru, having started with the arrival of the Spanish. It wasn't until the middle of the Nineteenth Century that the Italian contingent arrived. They influenced the general cooking agendas in the large cities with the addition of pasta, basil, and green and red sauces, among other things. Yet, local ideas modified the Italian tastes, as in this chicken dish.

3	whole skinless, boneless chicken breasts, halved
5	cloves garlic, ground to a paste with 2 tablespoons water
½	cup flour, or more if necessary
2	large eggs
2	teaspoons salt, or to taste
10	fresh cilantro leaves
½	cup corn oil for frying

1. Cut each halved chicken breast horizontally almost but not completely in half. You want to be able to open each piece up into a butterfly shape. Rub the chicken on both sides with the garlic paste.

2. Dip each chicken piece into the flour.

3. Beat together the eggs and salt. Stir in the cilantro leaves. Add the chicken to the egg mixture and let stand 10 minutes.

4. Heat the oil in a skillet large enough to hold the chicken. Add the chicken, cover, and fry it over low heat until light brown on both sides, about 4 minutes. Drain briefly on paper towels.

Serve warm, with rice or French fries and several salads. **Serves 6**

Gallina Enrollado (Callao)

BREAST OF CHICKEN ROLLS

*This elegant recipe is Chinese inspired, and one would expect
to find it in a Chifa restaurant in Lima rather than in other Peruvian
eating houses. Although a gallina is a large hen (see recipe title), a
moderate-sized chicken breast can be used.*

THE CHICKEN ROLLS

1	whole skinless breast of chicken, halved
1	teaspoon salt
⅛	teaspoon cinnamon
2	cloves garlic, ground to a paste with 2 tablespoons water
¼	teaspoon ginger, ground to a paste with a drop of water
2	eggs, beaten
2	thin slices boiled or baked ham, enough to cover each breast
	About 1 cup corn oil for deep-frying

1. Prepare the rolls: Pound each piece of chicken until ¼ inch thick. Rub the salt, cinnamon, and garlic and ginger pastes on both sides.

2. Dip the breasts in the beaten egg. Put a ham slice on each breast, then roll each breast up into cylinder. Tie with string at each end and in the middle. Dip the rolls into the egg once again.

3. Heat the oil in a wok or skillet until hot. Add the rolls and fry, turning them, over moderate heat for 3 minutes. Remove and set aside.

THE SAUCE

½	cup homemade chicken broth
¼	teaspoon sesame oil
8	snow peas
½	cup julienne slices red sweet pepper
2	scallions, sliced diagonally, 2 inches long
I	stalk celery heart, sliced thin on the diagonal
½	teaspoon ketchup
½	teaspoon soy sauce
¼	teaspoon sugar
I	tablespoon cornstarch dissolved in 3 tablespoons water

1. Prepare the sauce: Put the broth in a skillet. Add the sesame oil, snow peas, red pepper, scallions, celery, ketchup, soy sauce, and sugar and bring to a boil. Simmer over low heat for 2 minutes, then stir in just enough of the cornstarch mixture to lightly thicken the sauce.

2. Add the chicken rolls to the sauce and simmer them for 1 minute. Serve immediately.

Serve warm, with rice. **Serves 2**

Note: You can prepare multiples of the chicken rolls for more guests, but serve a modest amount of the sauce, only enough to bathe the rolls.

Gallina Enrollado con Salsa Tamarindo (Chinese)

CHICKEN ROLLS IN TAMARIND SAUCE

*Prepare the Chicken Rolls, then bathe them in the Tamarind Sauce with
Pineapple (page 212) instead of the sauce called for in the original recipe.
This is an unusually useful recipe for entertaining since one can prepare as
many chicken rolls as needed. Be sure to use only enough of the Tamarind
Sauce to coat the rolls. You do not want to drench them. Serve, with plain
white rice or with Arroz Chaufa Mixto, Fried Rice (page 142).*

Pollo al Pimento (Callao)

CHICKEN IN RED PEPPER SAUCE

Here is an old-time criolla *recipe that emphasizes sweet
red peppers, the botanical origin of which is Mexico, and very likely Peru,
as are the many varieties of the hot chili.*

1	teaspoon salt, or to taste
4	cloves garlic, ground to a paste with 2 tablespoons water
3	pounds chicken parts, leg, thigh, breast, loose skin and fat discarded, divided into 8 to 10 pieces
½	cup cornstarch
½	cup corn oil for deep-frying
1	medium onion, chopped (½ cup)
1	pound sweet red peppers (3), sliced
1	fresh yellow *aji amarillo*, seeded (yellow Peruvian chili, see Glossary) or 1 teaspoon dried yellow *aji* chili powder
1	pound potatoes, cooked in the skin, peeled and sliced lengthwise

1. Add the salt to the garlic paste and mix well. Rub the chicken pieces on all sides with the mixture. Then dust well with the cornstarch.

2. Heat the oil in a large skillet or wok and brown the chicken pieces over moderate heat for about 5 minutes, or until cooked through. Remove to paper towels to drain.

3. Pour off all but 1 tablespoon of the oil, add the onion, and stir-fry it over low heat for 1 minute. Add the fried chicken and combine.

4. In a food processor process the red peppers and *aji* to a smooth paste with ¼ cup water. Add this paste to the chicken mixture. Cover and simmer over low heat for 15 minutes, adding several tablespoons water if the sauce is too dry.

Serve warm, with rice and slices of boiled potatoes. **Serves 6 to 8**

Carapulcra con Sopa Seca (Chincha)
CHICKEN, PEANUTS, AND HOT CHILI

Carapulcra is a well-known hot-chili recipe from the Negro community of the city of Chincha, not too far from Lima. In addition to its idiosyncratic assembly and ingredients, it is served in combination with Sopa Seca, basil-flavored spaghetti.

Originally, Carapulcra was best made over a wood fire—how it is done in the Negro communities. There is this preoccupation with cooking over wood fires by the old-time Peruvians who remember the creole ambiance, the kitchens, clay cooking pots, and all the traditional methods that went with it.

Carapulcra and Sopa Seca are served together, in one plate, half and half. However, they may also be served separately, at different times.

6	cups water
3	pounds chicken parts, 8 pieces, loose skin and fat discarded
1	teaspoon salt, or to taste
3	or 4 dried *aji amarillo* (yellow Peruvian chili, see Glossary) or 1 to 2 teaspoons dried yellow *aji* chili powder
3	tablespoons corn oil
6	cloves garlic, chopped fine
¼	cup dry roasted peanuts, ground almost fine
1	teaspoon cumin
3	pounds whole potatoes, peeled, cooked, and cut into ½-inch cubes

1. Bring the water to a boil in a pan large enough to hold the chicken pieces and salt and simmer, covered, over low heat for ½ hour. Remove the chicken and set aside. Reserve the broth.

2. In a small pan simmer the whole hot chilies in ¼ cup water over low heat for 5 minutes. Let stand for 5 minutes, then process into a smooth paste. (If using chili powder, do not dissolve it.)

3. Heat the oil in the pan. Add the garlic and ground peanuts and stir-fry a moment to combine. Add the cumin and paste (or *aji* chili powder) and stir-fry over low heat for 1 minute.

4. Add the reserved chicken broth and bring to a boil. Add the potatoes and cook for 15 minutes. Return the chicken pieces to the pan to warm through. Adjust the salt if necessary.

Serve hot, with Sopa Seca (page 168). **Serves 8**

Sopa Seca (Chincha)

DRY SOUP (A PASTA)

Sopa seca literally means "dry soup"; in other words, it has no liquid. In fact, it is a pasta dish and is served by the Negro community with Carapulcra (preceding recipe). However, it can be served as an individual dish, too.

½   cup fresh basil leaves

1   tablespoon corn oil

2   cloves garlic, chopped fine

¼   teaspoon cumin

⅛   teaspoon pepper

½   cup ripe tomato, processed to a smooth paste

     Whole boneless skinless chicken breast, cooked and cut into 16 cubes

1   pound dried spaghetti (#8) broken into 4-inch pieces and cooked until *al dente*

2   tablespoons chopped parsley

1. Blanch the basil leaves in boiling water for 1 minute. Drain. In a food processor process the leaves to a smooth paste with ¼ cup water.

2. Heat the oil in a wide pan and stir-fry the garlic and cumin over low heat for ½ minute. Add the pepper and tomato paste and stir-fry another minute. Add the basil paste and stir to combine.

3. Add the chicken cubes and cooked spaghetti and stir-fry over low heat for 3 minutes to integrate all the flavors. Garnish with the parsley.

Serve hot, with or without Carapulcra. **Serves 8**

Aji de Gallina (Callao)
CHILI CHICKEN WITH WALNUTS

*Each region has its own culinary characteristics when it produces
a popular dish like this chili chicken. The title may be the same in other
preparations, but the flavor differs according to the unique preferences of
the region, in this case Callao near the capital city of Lima.*

4	cups (1 quart) water
2½	pounds boneless chicken parts, such as breast, thighs, and legs
2	fresh *aji amarillo* (yellow Peruvian chili, see Glossary), seeded; or 2 teaspoons dried yellow *aji* chili powder
4	cloves garlic
½	cup chopped onion
2	tablespoons walnuts
½	cup soda crackers, crushed
1	cup evaporated milk
¼	teaspoon dried oregano
1	teaspoon salt, or to taste
3	tablespoons corn oil
¼	teaspoon turmeric
2	tablespoons grated Parmesan cheese
1½	pounds potatoes (3), cooked in skin, peeled and sliced lengthwise
8	black olives
2	hard-boiled eggs, peeled and quartered

1. Bring the water to a boil in a large pot. Add the chicken pieces, and simmer over moderate heat for 20 minutes. Remove the chicken, cool, and tear into strips or threads. Reserve the broth.

2. In a food processor combine the *aji*, garlic, onion, and ¼ cup water and process to a paste. Remove to a bowl.

3. In the processor blend the walnuts, cracker crumbs, milk, oregano, and salt until smooth.

4. Heat the oil in a pan. Add the garlic and onion paste and stir-fry until golden over low heat. Add the turmeric and stir another minute.

5. Add 2 cups of the reserved broth, chicken strips, and Parmesan cheese and bring to a boil. Add the milk sauce and cook, stirring constantly over low heat for 5 minutes. It should be smooth and pourable. If too thick, add more broth until you have reached the desired consistency.

6. To serve, place the potato slices in the middle of a serving platter or individual plates. Pour the chili chicken with sauce over them. Garnish with the olives and eggs.

Serve at room temperature. **Serves 6 to 8.**

Caigua con Relleno de Pollo (Lambayeque)

CHICKEN-STUFFED CAIGUA

For information on caigua, *and possible substitutions for this green gourd, see page 117.*

8	medium sweet red or green peppers
2	cups water

THE STUFFING

I	pound skinless chicken breast
4	slices white bread, trim crusts, moistened with ¼ cup milk
I	egg, beaten
6	black olives, coarsely chopped
¼	cup raisins
I	hard-boiled egg, chopped
I	medium onion, sliced thin (½ cup)
½	teaspoon salt
¼	teaspoon pepper

THE CHICKEN BROTH SAUCE

1	tablespoon corn oil
¼	cup sliced onion
¼	cup chopped tomato
¼	teaspoon paprika
2	cloves garlic, ground to a paste with 2 tablespoons water
1	cup reserved chicken broth

1. Cut out a 2-inch round from the top of each pepper and remove the seeds and veins. Set aside.

2. Make the stuffing: Bring the water to a boil. Add the chicken breasts, cover the pan, and simmer over low heat for 15 minutes. Remove the chicken, cool well, and tear into threads. Reserve 1 cup of the broth.

3. In a bowl mix the chicken threads with the moistened bread, raw egg, olives, raisins, hard-boiled egg, onion, salt, and pepper.

4. Fill the peppers with the stuffing and replace the tops. (Should there be any stuffing left over, shape egg-sized balls and set aside.)

5. Make the sauce: Heat the oil in a skillet. Add the onion, tomato, paprika, and garlic paste and stir-fry over low heat for 3 minutes. Add the reserved chicken broth and bring to a boil.

6. Place the stuffed peppers in the sauce (with any balls from the leftover stuffing). Cover the skillet and simmer over low heat for 15 minutes.

Serve hot, with rice. **Serves 8**

Aji de Gallina (Chiclayo)

CHICKEN THREADS WITH ESCABECHE

Another classic dish as made in Chiclayo that includes white bread, crusts removed, moistened with chicken broth, then whipped into a creamy sauce. Peruvian cooking often surprises because it employs unexpected ingredients.

2	pounds whole boneless chicken breasts
4	cups (1 quart) water
1	teaspoon salt
½	pound loaf white bread, well trimmed of crust
3	tablespoons corn oil
1	clove garlic, ground to a paste with 2 tablespoons water
2	large onions, chopped fine (2 cups)
4	fresh *aji amarillo* (yellow Peruvian chili, see Glossary), seeded and processed into a paste; or 2 teaspoons dried yellow *aji* chili powder
1	cup evaporated milk or 1½ cups fresh milk
¼	teaspoon white pepper
10	lettuce leaves
1	pound potatoes (3), peeled, cooked until soft, and sliced lengthwise
4	hard-boiled eggs, peeled and quartered
8	black olives, pitted

1. Cook the chicken breasts in the water with the salt over moderate heat for 15 minutes. Remove the chicken and cool. Shred the chicken into 3-inch-long threads or pieces. Set aside. Reserve the broth.

2. In a bowl soak the bread in 2 cups of the reserved broth until soft; transfer to a food processor and process until creamy in texture.

3. Heat the oil in a large pan. Add the garlic paste, onions, and *aji* paste or powder and stir-fry over low heat for 2 minutes.

4. Add the bread mixture to the pan with the milk and mix together

well. Bring to a boil over low heat and cook, stirring continuously, for 10 minutes. Add the chicken and pepper and adjust the salt to taste.

To serve, arrange the lettuce on a platter or in a large bowl, top with the potato slices, and pour the creamed chicken over all. Garnish with the hard-boiled eggs and black olives in an attractive arrangement.

Serve warm. **Serves 8**

Chicharrón de Pollo (Arequipa)

CRISP FRIED BONELESS CHICKEN

Notice the Chinese influence in this justifiably popular (and tasty) chicken.
This is a modern preparation, with hardly any other era's influence.
The salad it is served with is another ensalada criolla.

1	**pound boneless chicken breast, cut into thumb-sized pieces**
1	**teaspoon soy sauce**
1	**teaspoon fresh lemon juice**
1	**clove garlic, ground to a paste with 2 tablespoons water**
½	**teaspoon salt**
⅛	**teaspoon pepper**
1	**teaspoon distilled white vinegar**
3	**tablespoons cornstarch**
1	**cup corn oil for deep-frying**
1	**pound potatoes, peeled and French fried (see Step 2, page 28)**
1	**large ripe tomato, cut into ½-inch cubes (1 cup)**
½	**cup thin-sliced onion**
1	**teaspoon red wine vinegar**
¼	**teaspoon salt**
¼	**teaspoon sugar**
2	**teaspoons chopped parsley**

1. Mix the chicken pieces with the soy sauce, lemon juice, garlic, salt, pepper, and vinegar. Let stand 15 minutes.

2. Dredge each piece of chicken in the cornstarch.

3. Heat the oil over moderate heat, then reduce the heat to low. Fry each piece of chicken, 1 at a time, turning for about 4 minutes, or until crispy. Drain briefly on paper towels.

4. Toss the tomato, onion, vinegar, salt, sugar, and parsley together to mix well.

Serve the chicken warm, with the French fries and the *ensalada criolla*.
Serves 4

Arroz Verde con Pollo (Trujillo)

GREEN RICE WITH CHICKEN

*The great Central Market of Trujillo is a model for the
quantity, quality, and variety of this region's traditional foodstuffs. In
addition, there are many eating booths that are clean as a whistle
and moderately priced. Throngs of shoppers stop by for their ceviche,
among other famous dishes. A generous portion of this Green Rice with
Chicken, served informally, would cost about $1.00.*

2	pounds chicken parts, cut into 8 generous pieces
1	teaspoon salt, or to taste
¼	teaspoon pepper
½	teaspoon cumin
¼	teaspoon dried oregano
3	tablespoons corn oil
2	cloves garlic, chopped fine
1	medium onion, chopped (½ cup)
1	tomato, chopped (½ cup)
¼	teaspoon turmeric
1	teaspoon dried yellow *aji* chili powder (see **Glossary**)
6	cups water
½	fresh or frozen green peas
1	carrot, diced into ¼-inch cubes (½ cup)
3	cups rice, well rinsed, soaked in water to cover ½ hour, and drained
¼	cup chopped fresh cilantro

1. Spoon the chicken with salt, pepper, cumin, and oregano and let stand for 15 minutes.

2. Put the oil in a pan large enough to hold the chicken. Add the garlic, onion, tomato, turmeric, and *aji* powder and stir-fry over low heat for 2 minutes. Add the chicken and fry on both sides for a total of 15 minutes. Remove the chicken and set aside.

3. Add the water to the pan, bring it to a boil, and add the peas, carrot, and rice; mix well to color the rice. Return the chicken to the pan, stir again, and simmer, covered, for 15 to 20 minutes.

Serve warm, with a simple salad. **Serves 6 to 8**

Sajta de Pollo (Puno)
SPECIAL CHICKEN IN PEANUT SAUCE

Sajta is not an everyday dish for family cooks. It is reserved more for special events and celebrations. The combination of ingredients is unconventional—assorted vegetables, yellow aji *chili, cheese, and toasted peanuts—but they come together nicely in this fine preparation.*

3 ½   **pound chicken, loose skin and fat discarded, cut into 8 pieces**

4   **cups (I quart) water**

¼   **teaspoon cumin**

3   **cloves garlic, chopped**

I   **teaspoon salt, or to taste**

I   **medium onion, chopped (½ cup)**

4   **teaspoons dried yellow** *aji* **chili powder (see Glossary)**

½   **cup dry roasted peanuts, coarsely ground**

½   **cup chopped** *queso fresco* **(see Glossary) or Feta cheese**

¼   **cup plain dry bread crumbs**

½   **cup milk**

2   **tablespoons corn oil**

I   **pound small potatoes (8), peeled, boiled until tender, and drained**

½   **cup fresh or frozen green peas, lightly cooked**

2   **tablespoons chopped parsley**

1. Put the chicken in a pan with 3½ cups of the water. Add the cumin, garlic, salt, ¼ cup chopped onion, and *aji* chili powder. Cook over low heat for ½ hour, or until the chicken is tender. Remove and reserve 1 cup broth.

2. In a food processor blend the peanuts, cheese, bread crumbs, milk, and remaining ¼ cup onion until smooth.

3. Heat the oil in a pan, add the peanut mixture, and cook the sauce over low heat for 10 minutes.

4. To serve, arrange the chicken pieces in the middle of a serving platter. If the peanut sauce seems too thick, dilute it with some of the reserved broth. Place the potatoes, carrots, and peas around the chicken. Then pour the sauce over all. Garnish with the parsley.

Serve warm. **Serves 8**

Escabeche de Pollo (Trujillo)

SPICY CHICKEN SALAD

I liked the large, clean, well-lighted (with skylights) public markets in Peru. In Trujillo, where this popular recipe comes from, I located a home cook in her stall who specialized in Escabeche de Pollo, a true criollo *dish, and a large pot of noodle broth, which she gave as a complimentary bowl to her regular customers.*

The salad was excellent, a grandmother's recipe, which I had no qualms about eating as I sat on a wooden bench with other shoppers/diners, using a roll of bathroom tissue (as much as you wanted) as a table napkin. One can learn a lot about the country, the food, and the cost of living at such a place. No politics!

A whole 3-pound chicken, well rinsed and loose skin and fat discarded

2	**teaspoons salt**
¼	**teaspoon pepper**
1	**large carrot, cut into 3-inch lengths**
5	**cups water**
2	**fresh *aji amarillo* (yellow Peruvian chili, see Glossary), seeded and sliced thin lengthwise; or 1 teaspoon dried yellow *aji* chili powder**
1	**pound large onions, peeled and sliced but not too thin**
2	**to 3 tablespoons white wine vinegar, to taste**
½	**teaspoon turmeric**
1	**teaspoon cumin**
2	**tablespoons corn oil**
2	**cloves garlic, chopped fine**
1	**teaspoon dried oregano**
2	**pounds yuca (see Glossary), peeled, cut into large thumb-sized pieces, and cooked, for serving**
6	**lettuce leaves**
6	**black olives, pitted**
3	**hard-boiled eggs, peeled and halved**

1. Put the chicken, salt, pepper, carrot, and water in a pot, cover, and bring the water to a boil over moderate heat. Cook for ½ hour, or until the chicken is tender. Remove the chicken and carrot and set aside. (Reserve 1 cup of broth and reduce it to ½ cup over moderate heat.) Cool the chicken, cut into 6 pieces, and discard the skin.

2. Blanch the onions in the hot broth for a few seconds. Transfer into a large mixing bowl. Add the vinegar, turmeric, cumin, and fresh *aji* slices or powder.

3. Heat the oil in a skillet. Add the garlic and oregano and stir-fry over moderate heat for 1 minute. Add to the vinegar mixture.

4. Add the chicken pieces and the ½ cup reduced broth. Taste the mixture and adjust the salt.

Arrange the lettuce leaves on a serving platter or on individual plates. Spoon the chicken and sauce in the center of the platter and put the yuca slices around the edge. Garnish with the olives and hard-boiled eggs.

Serve at room temperature or cool. **Serves 6**

Tallarin de Pollo (Arequipa)

SPAGHETTI AND CHICKEN

The Italian community has had a popular influence on the cooking of Peru. Various spaghetti dishes with a Peruvian touch have entered the mainstream and differ from the Italian food that we recognize in the United States. This dish is a good example.

1	pound dried spaghetti (#8)
2	teaspoons salt
3	tablespoons corn oil
1	teaspoon finely chopped seeded fresh *aji amarillo* (yellow Peruvian chili, see Glossary) or 1 teaspoon dried yellow *aji* chili powder
5	cloves garlic, ground to a paste with 2 tablespoons water
¼	teaspoon cumin
5	whole peppercorns
3	bay leaves
1	teaspoon dried oregano
2	dried Chinese mushrooms, soaked in water until soft, drained, and sliced
1½	cups chopped peeled tomatoes, processed to a paste
1	cup sliced onion, processed to a paste
3	cups water
2	pounds chicken legs (8 to 10)
⅓	cup grated Parmesan cheese, for serving

1. Cook the pasta in enough water with 1 teaspoon salt and 1 tablespoon oil until *al dente,* about 10 minutes. Drain, rinse under cold water, and set aside in a steamer to keep warm.

2. Heat the remaining 2 tablespoons oil in a pan. Add the *aji* chili and stir-fry over low heat a few seconds. Add the garlic paste, cumin, peppercorns, bay leaves, oregano, and mushrooms and stir-fry for 1 minute.

3. Push the tomato and onion pastes through a metal sieve into the pan and add the water. Bring to a boil.

4. Now add the chicken legs. Cover the pan and cook over low heat until the chicken is tender, about 25 minutes. (If the sauce seems too thin, reduce it by cooking, uncovered, for 10 to 15 minutes.)

Serve the spaghetti in the center of individual plates. Top it with 1 chicken leg and pour the sauce over all. Sprinkle with Parmesan cheese.

Serve hot. **Serves 6 to 8**

Pebre de Tres Carnes (Arequipa)
STEW OF THREE MEATS

Pebre is generally served on Semana Santa, Easter. It is a long-held tradition that may extend back to the Spanish colonial era.

4	cups (1 quart) water
¾	pound boneless chicken, cut into 6 pieces
¾	pound boneless beef, cut into 6 pieces
¾	pound lamb ribs, cut into 6 pieces
3	white *chuno*, halved (see Glossary, optional)
2	cloves garlic, crushed
1	teaspoon salt, or to taste
¾	pound potato, peeled and cut into 6 pieces
2	tablespoons rice
4	whole allspice
1	sprig mint
¼	cup cooked chick peas

1. Bring the water to a boil over moderate heat in a large pan. Add the 3 meats and cook, covered, for ½ hour.

2. Add the *chuno* (if used), garlic, salt, potato, rice, allspice, and mint and simmer over low heat for ½ hour, or until the meats are tender. Add the chick peas and cook another 2 minutes. Adjust the salt.

Serve hot, with rice and salads. **Serves 6**

Pollo Saltado Estilo Japones

STIR-FRIED CHICKEN JAPANESE STYLE

*The small Japanese community brought their culinary
ideas to Peru and added them to what they found there. Here is a stir-fry
of boneless breast of chicken, assorted vegetables, and seasonings
that reveals the transfer from Japan to Peru.*

2½ pounds boneless skinless breast of chicken

1 tablespoon corn oil

2 cups sliced celery hearts (2-inch-long pieces cut on diagonal)

2 cups sliced large onions

2 cups sliced sweet red pepper (2-inch-long pieces)

3 cups shredded Napa Chinese cabbage (cut ¼ inch thick)

4 scallions, cut into 1-inch pieces

2 teaspoons chopped ginger

4 cloves garlic, chopped

⅛ teaspoon pepper

3 tablespoons oyster sauce

3 tablespoons black soy sauce

2 tablespoons white vinegar

1 tablespoon sesame oil

1. Cut the chicken into 2-inch-long thin slices. Heat the corn oil in a wok. Add the chicken to the wok and stir-fry over moderate heat for 1 minute. Remove and set aside.

2. Add all the vegetables—celery, onions, red pepper, Napa cabbage, scallions, ginger, and garlic—and stir-fry for 2 minutes. Return chicken to wok.

3. Add the soy sauce, vinegar, and sesame oil and continue to stir-fry for 3 minutes to integrate all the flavors. If the mixture seems too dry, stir in 2 tablespoons water.

Serve hot, with rice. **Serves 6**

Escabeche de Gallina (Cuzco)

PICKLED HEN WITH VEGETABLES

One of the most attractive dishes in Peru. I went to the public market in Cuzco every day about noon to visit the kiosk that specialized in this dish to take yet another lesson. The wine vinegar was made in Ica, the grape-growing region of Peru; the homegrown fat hens were preferred to the scrawny chickens and the vegetables were grown without all the harmful chemicals.

THE HEN

4	cups water
3½	pounds hen parts, such as breast, thigh, leg, divided into 16 pieces and skinned
2	carrots, sliced
2	tablespoons sliced onion
1	clove garlic, crushed
1	stalk celery, halved
1	small leek, halved and well rinsed
½	teaspoon salt

4   black peppercorns

1   teaspoon dried oregano

Prepare the hen: Bring the water to a boil in a large pot. Add the hen and all the remaining ingredients and cook, covered, over low heat for ½ hour, or until the hen is tender. Remove and strain the broth. Cook the broth until it has been reduced to 1 cup. Refrigerate overnight and discard the firm layer of fat on top. Reserve.

THE VEGETABLES

1   **pound cauliflower, cut into 2-inch florets**

2   **large carrots, sliced diagonally**

½   **pound green beans, cut into 2-inch pieces**

2   **pounds small white onions, peeled**

Prepare the vegetables: Cook the cauliflower, carrots, beans, and onions separately until firmly soft, *al dente*. Drain and set aside.

THE SAUCE

¼   **cup white wine vinegar, to taste**

1   **teaspoon salt**

1   **teaspoon sugar**

⅛   **teaspoon pepper**

¼   **cup corn or olive oil**

1   **teaspoon sliced seeded fresh *aji amarillo* (yellow Peruvian chili, see Glossary)**

1   **cup reserved reduced chicken broth**

1. To assemble the Escabeche: Mix the vinegar, salt, sugar, pepper, oil and *aji* chili together well.

2. One day before you intend to serve the Escabeche, mix all the vegetables together with the hen. Add the vinegar sauce and the 1 cup reserved broth. Cover and marinate overnight in the refrigerator.

To serve, place the hen pieces in the center of a large platter. Space the vegetables all around the perimeter. Pour the marinade over all.

Serve cold. **Serves 8**

Parrillada de Huevo de Cordoniz (Iquitos)

QUAIL EGGS AND CHICKEN STIR-FRY

The Amazon region boasted of a fine Chifa restaurant in the middle of nowhere. A Chinese meal was refreshing after many days of concentrating on criollo *dishes.*

1	tablespoon corn oil
1	clove garlic, crushed
	A ½-inch piece of ginger, crushed
3	pieces celery, each 2 inches long
1	cup shredded cabbage
1	cup shredded bok choy
1	teaspoon dried yellow *aji* chili powder (see Glossary, optional)
15	quail eggs, fresh or canned, cooked
15	large cube cooked chicken, white and dark meat
1	teaspoon soy sauce
½	teaspoon sugar
1	teaspoon salt, or to taste

1. Heat the oil in a wok or large skillet. Add the garlic and ginger and stir-fry over moderate heat for 2 minutes. Add the celery, cabbage, bok choy and *aji* (if used) and stir-fry for 3 minutes.

2. Add the quail eggs, cooked chicken, soy sauce, sugar, and salt and stir-fry for 3 minutes to combine and heat through.

Serve warm, with rice and other Chifa dishes. **Serves 6 to 8**

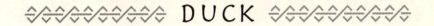

DUCK

Pato Saltado a La Paisana (Chiclayo)

DUCK AND VEGETABLES PEASANT STYLE

*Peruvians believe that duck has a certain cachet, that it is
something special, better than the everyday chicken, which can be eaten
everywhere and anytime. This recipe is a winner. A final note: Humitas
(page 16) are often served as an* entrada, *appetizer, with this.*

	A young duckling, 3 to 4 pounds, loose skin and fat discarded, cut into 10 pieces
2	teaspoons salt, or to taste
¼	teaspoon pepper
½	teaspoon cumin
4	cloves garlic, ground to a paste with 2 tablespoons water
2	teaspoons red wine vinegar
2	tablespoons corn oil
2	teaspoons paprika
2	cups fresh or frozen green peas
1	cup carrot sticks (little-finger-sized)
1	large sweet red or green pepper (little-finger-sized)
2	fresh *aji amarillo* (yellow Peruvian chili, see Glossary), seeded and sliced lengthwise
2	ripe tomatoes, cut into strips (2 cups)
½	cup water

1. Mix the duckling, salt, pepper, cumin, garlic paste, and vinegar together, cover, and marinate for 3 hours.

2. Heat the oil in a large pan. Add the duckling, marinade, and paprika and stir-fry over low heat for 15 minutes to brown.

3. Now add the peas, carrots, red or green pepper, *aji,* tomatoes, water, cover the pan, and cook for 1 hour, which is enough to

tenderize the duckling and produce a thick sauce. (If too dry, stir in about ¼ cup water.)

Serve warm, with rice. **Serves 10**

Guiso de Pato (Lambayeque)

DUCK IN THICK RED SAUCE

Every region and community in Peru has their own combinations for producing similar dishes. They are never the same. This duck was prepared for me in a town near Chiclayo.

1	duck, 4½ to 5 pounds, loose skin and fat discarded, cut into 8 pieces
1	teaspoon salt, or to taste
¼	teaspoon pepper
1	tablespoon corn oil
3	cloves garlic, chopped fine
2	large onions, chopped (2 cups)
1	sweet red pepper, sliced (1 cup)
1	large tomato, chopped (1 cup)
2	teaspoons cumin
2	teaspoons paprika
2	tablespoons red wine vinegar
2	cups water
2	cups fresh or frozen green peas

1. Season the duck with salt and pepper. Heat the oil in a large pan. Add the duck pieces and brown them over low heat for 15 minutes. Considerable fat will accumulate; pour it off. Return the duck to the pan.

2. Now add all the remaining ingredients, except the peas, to the pan with the duck and bring to a boil. Cover the pan and cook over low heat for about 1 hour.

3. Add the peas and cook for 10 minutes. The duck should be tender and the sauce thick.

Serve warm, with rice and Ensalada Mixta (page 214). **Serves 8**

Arroz con Pato (Trujillo)

DUCK WITH RICE

On the outer edge of the northern city of Trujillo is what is known as the circuito del pato, *the duck circuit. This is a dusty road twisting for about a mile off a main street with one large garden restaurant after another. The specialty that attracts hundreds of diners on the weekend is duck,* el pato, *or the male duck, which can weigh 7 or 8 pounds and has thick firm meat with a layer of fat. And the most popular family-style method of preparing the farm-raised duck is this recipe.*

1	duck 4½ pounds, loose skin and fat discarded, cut into 10 pieces
1	teaspoon salt, or to taste
¼	teaspoon pepper
¼	teaspoon cumin
7	cups water
3	tablespoons corn oil
2	cloves garlic, chopped
2	tablespoons chopped onion
½	cup diced carrot (¼-inch pieces)
½	cup fresh or frozen green peas
¼	cup fresh corn kernels
2	tablespoons chopped cilantro
¼	teaspoon turmeric
½	teaspoon paprika
1	cup beer
3	cups rice, well rinsed, soaked in water to cover ½ hour, and drained

1. Season the duck pieces with the salt, pepper, and cumin. Put the duck in a large pan with 1 cup of the water, bring to a boil, and cover. Cook over low heat until the water has evaporated. Add the oil and stir-fry the duck for 5 minutes.

2. Remove the duck to a plate. Add the garlic, onion, carrot, green peas, corn, cilantro, turmeric, and paprika to the pan, mix well, and fry over low heat for 5 minutes.

3. Add the remaining 6 cups water and the beer and return the duck to the pan. Bring to a boil and add the rice. Cover and simmer over low heat for 15 to 20 minutes. Just before serving, stir gently to combine.

Serve warm, with salads of your choice or your favorite Zarza (see Index). **Serves 10**

Arroz con Pato (Chiclayo)
DUCK WITH SEASONED RICE

Peruvians like chicken, but admire the ducks that waddle in their gardens. In addition, there are many duck recipes in the cooking of the countryside. In fact, duck is probably the most popular but costly type of poultry. Duck with seasoned rice leads the list.

3	tablespoons corn oil
1	duck, 4 pounds, loose skin and fat discarded, cut into 8 pieces
1	medium onion, chopped (½ cup)
4	cloves garlic, chopped
1	sweet green pepper, chopped (1 cup)

¼	cup diced peeled *zapallo* (see Glossary) or butternut squash
¼	teaspoon cumin
2	teaspoons salt, or to taste
¼	teaspoon pepper
20	sprigs fresh cilantro processed to a paste with 2 tablespoons water
½	cup dark beer
1	carrot, cut into ¼-inch dice (½ cup)
¼	cup fresh or frozen green peas
7	cups water
3	cups rice, well rinsed, soaked in water to cover ½ hour, and drained

1. Heat the oil in a large deep pan and brown the duck pieces on all sides over low heat for 10 minutes. Remove the duck pieces and set aside.

2. Add the onion, garlic, green pepper, squash, cumin, salt, pepper, cilantro paste, beer, carrots, and green peas to the pan and stir-fry the mixture for 3 minutes. Add the water and bring to a boil.

3. Return the duck to the pan, cover, and cook until tender, about 1 hour.

4. Add the rice, cover, and simmer over low heat for about 15 minutes, or until the rice is cooked. Stir well to combine, cover the pan, and remove it from the heat. Let stand 10 minutes before serving. Adjust the salt if necessary.

Serve warm. **Serves 8**

Arroz con Pato al Estilo Chiclayano (Chiclayo)

CHILI DUCK WITH RICE FROM CHICLAYO

A variation on the theme of the much-loved classic dish,
spiced duck, this time cooked together with rice. It is customary to serve
a favorite ceviche as an appetizer to this dish.

	A 4-pound duck cut into 10 pieces
1	teaspoon dried yellow *aji* chili powder (see Glossary)
20	sprigs fresh cilantro, sliced
2	large onions, chopped (1½ cups)
4	cloves garlic, ground to a paste with 2 tablespoons water
1	teaspoon salt, or to taste
¼	teaspoon pepper
½	teaspoon turmeric
1	cup light beer
9	cups water
4	cups rice, well rinsed, soaked in water to cover ½ hour, and drained
2	cups fresh or frozen green peas

1. Heat the oil in a pan large enough to hold the duck easily. Add the duck and stir-fry over low heat for 15 minutes to brown. Add the chili powder, cilantro, onions, garlic paste, salt, pepper, and turmeric and stir-fry for 5 minutes. Add the beer, cover the pan, and cook for 15 minutes.

2. Add the water, bring it to a boil, and cook the duck until it is tender, about 45 minutes. Add the rice and peas and combine well. Cover the pan and cook over low heat for 15 to 20 minutes. The rice will absorb the liquid. Stir again to combine.

Serve warm. **Serves 10**

Escabeche de Pato (Lima)

PICKLED DUCK SALAD

*Vinegar is the predominant flavor in this dish, contrasting sharply
with the characteristic gamy flavor of the duck. All over the country Peruvians
enjoy duck, especially so when it is pickled with red wine vinegar from the
well-established wine and pisco industry in the region of Ica.*

*This can be eaten hot or cold. I prefer it hot. And some people prefer it for
breakfast—a possibility that I have not yet considered.*

8	cups (2 quarts) water
1	duck, 5 to 6 pounds, loose skin and fat discarded cut into 8 serving pieces
2	teaspoons salt, or to taste
4	cloves garlic, ground to a paste with 2 tablespoons water
4	tablespoons corn oil
1	tablespoon paprika chili
¼	teaspoon pepper
½	teaspoon cumin
1½	pounds red onions, cut into thick slices, blanched briefly in boiling water, and drained
½	cup red wine vinegar
1	fresh yellow *aji amarillo* (yellow Peruvian chili, see Glossary), seeded and sliced lengthwise
	Lettuce leaves
4	hard-boiled eggs, peeled and halved
16	black olives, pitted
1	large sweet potato, cooked, peeled, and sliced, for serving

1. Bring the water to a boil in a large pot. Add the duck pieces, salt, and
half the garlic paste. Cover and cook over medium heat for 1 to 1½ hours,
or until the duck is tender. (Duck is a firm meat that requires extended
cooking.) Remove the duck and set aside. Discard the cooking liquid.

2. Heat 2 tablespoons of the oil in a pan. Add the remaining garlic paste, pepper, and cumin and stir-fry over low heat for 1 minute. Add the blanched onions. Fry the mixture, stirring, for 3 minutes.

3. Stir in the vinegar and *aji* and bring to a boil. Remove from the heat and keep warm.

4. Heat the remaining 2 tablespoons oil in a large skillet. Add the duck pieces and brown them over moderate heat for 5 minutes.

To serve, line a serving platter with the lettuce. Place the fried duck pieces in the center and pour the vinegar sauce over them. Garnish with the hard-boiled eggs, olives, and slices of sweet potato, placing them around the perimeter of the platter.

Serve with white rice or bread. **Serves 8**

Pato Asado Estilo La Selva (Iquitos)

ROAST DUCK JUNGLE STYLE

Here is a popular family-style method of preparing duck in the Amazonian region. It was in the city of Iquitos that I learned this recipe.

1	duck, 4 pounds, loose skin and fat discarded, cut into 8 pieces
2	tablespoons corn oil
½	teaspoon turmeric
3	cloves garlic, ground to a paste with 2 tablespoons water
2	bay leaves
2	teaspoons salt
⅛	teaspoon nutmeg
½	teaspoon cumin
1	ripe large plantain, peeled, yellow/black skin, and cut diagonally into 8 slices
1½	cups water

1. In a large skillet stir-fry the duck in the oil with the turmeric over moderate heat for 10 minutes. Add the garlic paste, bay leaves, salt, nutmeg, and cumin and mix well to combine.

2. Cover the pan and allow the steam to produce some liquid in the pan. Add the plantain slices. Since duck is a firm-fleshed bird, add the water. Simmer, covered, over low heat for about 1 hour, or until the duck is tender. There should be a small amount of sauce.

Serve warm, with rice and Salsa Criolla (page 138). **Serves 8**

Guiso del Pato (Trujillo)

DUCK STEW

The many large outdoor restaurants that line the dirt road of the "duck circuit" on the edge of Trujillo city feature the pato *(male) or the* pata *(female) duck, which is a smaller bird but not necessarily more tender. Peruvian cooks prefer the large, fat, and very meaty* pato, *with its firm-fleshed meat that requires a sharp knife and strong teeth. But these free-range, family-raised ducks have a natural flavor that is worth the extra energy you need to use for additional chewing and tugging.*

2½	pounds duck parts, cut into 8 portions, fat removed
1	teaspoon salt, or to taste
1	teaspoon paprika
1	teaspoon cumin
1	teaspoon dried oregano
4	cloves garlic, ground to a paste with 2 tablespoons water
1	tablespoon finely chopped seeded fresh *aji amarillo* (yellow Peruvian chili, see Glossary) or 1 teaspoon dried yellow *aji* chili powder
2	tablespoons chopped cilantro
3	tablespoons corn oil
2	cups water
1	cup dark beer
1	medium onion, sliced (½ cup)

1. Season the duck pieces with the salt, paprika, cumin, oregano, garlic paste, *aji*, and cilantro and set aside 15 minutes.

2. Heat the oil in a wide pan and fry the duck with its marinade, covered, over low heat for 10 minutes. Add the water, beer, and onion and bring to a boil. Cover the pan and simmer for 45 minutes, or until the duck is tender. (Should the sauce be too thick, add an additional ½ cup water.)

Serve warm, with rice, boiled yuca, and a favorite hot sauce. **Serves 8**

Higados de Pato Saltado (Trujillo)

DUCK LIVER SAUTÉ

There are plenty of ducks in the markets of Peru, fat and freshly slaughtered.
They have been fed on country grains, grass, and water; their livers are well
flavored with natural foods rather than with the artificial feed in commercial lots.
A touch of wine vinegar and slices of onion and tomato invigorate the taste of this
duck liver sauté. Chicken livers can be prepared in exactly the same way.

2	tablespoons corn oil
1	pound duck liver, cut into quarters
½	teaspoon salt
¼	teaspoon pepper
¼	teaspoon paprika
2	teaspoons red wine vinegar
⅓	cup sliced onion
⅓	cup sliced tomato

1. Heat the oil in a skillet. Add the liver, salt, pepper, paprika, and vinegar and stir-fry over moderate heat for 3 minutes.

2. Add the onion and tomato slices and stir-fry for 3 minutes. The liver should be lightly sautéed and tender. If you prefer well-done duck liver, cook for 2 minutes more.

Serve warm, with boiled potatoes, sliced lengthwise, or white rice.
Serves 6

OTHER POULTRY

Pepian de Pavo (Chiclayo)

TURKEY STEW IN PEANUT SAUCE

*Turkey is one of the lesser meats of Peru; that is to say, it is not frequently
prepared. One of the elderly ladies in Chiclayo, who was a mine of information
about the regional foods, provided me with this unconventional recipe.*

3	pounds boneless light and dark turkey meat, cut into 8 pieces
1	tablespoon salt
2	tablespoons corn oil
1	medium onion, chopped (½ cup)
1	ripe tomato, chopped (½ cup)
5	cloves garlic, ground to a paste with 2 tablespoons water
¼	teaspoon pepper
2	teaspoons paprika
6	cups hot water
½	cup chick pea flour (see Note)
½	cup dry roasted peanuts, ground medium-fine but still with some texture

1. Rub the turkey pieces with the salt and set aside for 15 minutes.

2. Heat the oil in a large wide pan. Add the onion and tomato and stir-
fry over low heat 3 minutes. Add the garlic paste, pepper, and paprika
and fry for 2 minutes. Add the turkey pieces and cook them over low
heat for 5 minutes until lightly browned all over.

3. Add the hot water, bring it to a boil, and simmer the mixture for ½
hour, or until the turkey is tender. Add the chick pea flour and ground
peanuts and stir continuously for 10 minutes to integrate the flavors

and textures. The sauce is thick, and may become too thick, in which case add about ½ cup more hot water; mix well. Adjust the salt.

Serve warm, with white rice. **Serves 8**

Note: Chick pea flour can be purchased in East Indian shops under the name of besan. Or you can prepare it yourself by toasting ½ cup dried chick peas in a nonstick pan until they are light brown; cool and grind to a powder in a food processor.

The dry roasted peanuts should be ground to a powder, too, but not so fine that it does not have a modicum of texture.

Pavo Relleno Deshuesado (Arequipa)

BONELESS STUFFED TURKEY

*Turkey is sometimes prepared in Peru but is not a popular bird, widely
outdistanced by duck and chicken. This stupendous stuffed turkey was served
to me at one of the outstanding picanterias in Arequipa. It was a beautiful
sunny day and I was sitting in a large outdoor patio that was eons away
from the original picanterias that were rundown "beer joints," where
traditional food and drinks were served.*

*I have made many boneless chickens, from the cuisines of
Morocco, Indonesia, and Guatemala. The stuffings were all different
but the technique of boning poultry is the same.*

A 10-pound turkey, boned (see Note)

¼	**cup corn oil**
¾	**pound ground beef**
¾	**pound ground lamb**
¾	**pound ground chicken**
¾	**pound ground pork**
5	**cloves garlic, ground to a paste with 2 tablespoons water**
1	**teaspoon cumin**
¼	**teaspoon nutmeg**
2	**teaspoons salt, or to taste**
1	**teaspoon pepper**
2	**tablespoons raisins**
3	**dried figs, soaked in water for 4 hours, drained, and cut into ¼-inch dice**
1	**large carrot, cut into ¼-inch dice (1 cup)**
¼	**cup fresh or frozen green peas**
4	**slices bread, crusts removed, soaked in ½ cup milk until soft**
4	**hard-boiled eggs, peeled**
2	**tablespoons butter**

1. Heat the oil in a large wide pan, add the 4 meats, garlic paste, cumin, nutmeg, salt, pepper, raisins, figs, carrot, peas, and soaked bread and stir-fry over low heat for 10 minutes to partially cook the meat and integrate all the seasonings and ingredients. Cool.

2. Sew up the neck end of the boneless turkey, then begin to fill the cavity, adding the whole hard-boiled eggs, 1 at a time, as the cavity fills. Sew up the tail end firmly.

3. Rub the turkey with 1 tablespoon of the butter and the roasting pan with the remaining 1 tablespoon butter. Place the turkey in the roasting pan, breast up, cover, and roast in a preheated 350 degree oven for ½ hour. Uncover the pan and continue to roast until the turkey is crisp brown, for 1 hour more.

If serving it warm, let the turkey rest for ½ hour before slicing. Or, cool it completely, refrigerate, and slice cold. **Serves 20, or more, with a variety of Peruvian salads and side dishes.**

Note: In the interests of time, ask your butcher to bone a 10-pound turkey (or oven-stuffer hen) and have him remove the legs and the first two joints of the wings, which are not included in this preparation.

Guiso de Pichones (Lambayeque)

PIGEONS IN RED SAUCE

We bought pigeons in the public market for this guiso.
In New York I buy them cleaned and presentable in Chinatown,
where they are always available.

Cornish game hens are a fair enough substitute, but use two hens,
since they are larger than pigeons.

2	tablespoons corn oil
4	pigeons, cleaned, each cut into 4 pieces
I	carrot, cut into ½-inch cubes (¾ cup)
I	medium ripe tomato, chopped fine (½ cup)
I	small onion, chopped fine (⅓ cup)
I	sweet red pepper, chopped fine (¾ cup)
I	teaspoon salt, or to taste
I	teaspoon cumin
¼	teaspoon pepper
I	teaspoon paprika
3	cloves garlic, chopped fine
I	cup water
2	teaspoons red wine vinegar
I½	cups fresh or frozen green peas
½	pound (I) potato, peeled and cut into ¼-inch cubes

1. In a large wide pan heat the oil. Add the pigeon pieces and cook, turning, until lightly browned all over.

2. Add all the remaining ingredients, except the peas and potato, and combine well. Cook over low heat for 40 minutes. Add the peas and potato and cook, covered, for 15 minutes more. Should the liquid evaporate too quickly, add another ½ cup water and cook until the pigeons are tender and the sauce thick.

Serve warm, with white rice. **Serves 6 or 7**

Estofada de Choca (Lake Titicaca)

STEWED CHOCA

A choca is a black feathered aquatic bird found on Lake Titicaca on the border of Peru and Bolivia.

A serviceable launch was taking a small number of people from Punto to visit the floating islands on the lake that are inhabited by the Uros Indians who speak the Aymara language. The Uros have been there a long time; they are isolated and poor with their aquatic way of life as fishermen and hunters.

The choca *is snared in the rushes that abound on the islands and provide food as well as firm grass for the Uros who use it to build their homes. I was able to buy a* choca *from one of the Indians for 80 cents and took it back to the cook at my hotel to prepare. It tastes very much like the dark meat of chicken.* Choca *is a firm-fleshed bird. The cook, in fact, used a pressure cooker—a popular kitchen tool in Peru for extra-firm meat.*

I	wild *choca* from Lake Titicaca (see Note)
I	tablespoon corn oil
I	medium onion, chopped (½ cup)
3	cloves garlic, chopped
¾	cup fresh tomatoes, peeled and puréed
I	potato, peeled and cut into 6 pieces (I cup)
I	carrot, sliced diagonally into 6 pieces
I	teaspoon salt, or to taste
6	whole peppercorns
¼	teaspoon cumin
¼	cup fresh or frozen green peas
2	cups water

1. Clean the *choca* (or wild duck of your choice), pluck the feathers, eviscerate, and rinse well. Cut the *choca* into 6 pieces, a total weight of about 1 pound.

2. Heat the oil in a pan. Add the onion and garlic and stir-fry over low heat for 2 minutes. Add the tomatoes and stir-fry for 3 minutes.

3. Now add the *choca*, potato, carrot, salt, peppercorns, cumin, peas, and water. Bring to a boil, cover the pan, and cook for about 45 minutes, or until the *choca* is tender and the sauce is thick.

Serve hot, with rice. **Serves 6**

Note: Rabbit, about 1½ pounds, may also be prepared utilizing the same ingredients.

COREGIMIENTO
Q EL COREG.ᵒ² COИBIDA

en su mesa alos menagentes vaja y ñ mi tayo a mes tizo mulato y le to ria

mestizo

mulato

corregidor

probicias

SAUCES, SALADS AND VEGETABLE DISHES

One of the most ubiquitous sights in Peruvian restaurants is the bowl of the Salsa Criolla (Creole Onion Condiment) on the tables. It is not a sauce but a Zarza, or side dish, that might be called a chutney in India. It is designed to supplement the flavors of the meal and comes in a variety of combinations. It is this group of table side dishes that are needed and wanted by Peruvian diners. Many but not all are vegetarian. Hot (spicy) sauces as well as mixed salads enlarge the scope of what appears on the table. They make family dining more interesting, even when the larder is not bulging with food.

Peruvians are not dedicated vegetarians as some other nationalities are. They generally do not confine themselves to a nonmeat diet unless it is a private decision. Often as not, it might be an economic decision, since meat could be too expensive. Yet there are a number of preparations that are vegetarian that elicit great culinary interest and are very popular, such as the famous Papa a la Huancaina (Potatoes in a Cheese Sauce) or the equally well-known Tallarines en Salsa Verde (Spaghetti in a Green Sauce). There are others in the regional countryside, many with the historic potato, that enrich the cuisine at very little cost.

In sum, salads, spicy sauces, and side dishes are a tastefully useful category of Peruvian home cooking.

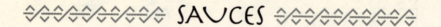

Salsa Criolla, Zarza (All Peru)

CREOLE ONION CONDIMENT

This is probably the most common table condiment throughout Peru—not a sauce at all. It is also frequently called Zarza.

2	**medium red onions, sliced thin (1 cup)**
4	**tablespoons fresh lime juice**
¼	**teaspoon distilled white vinegar**
1	**teaspoon olive oil**
1	**teaspoon chopped fresh cilantro**
⅛	**teaspoon salt, or to taste**

Rinse the onion well in cold water and pat dry with paper towels. In a medium bowl mix all the ingredients together and serve immediately.

Serve at room temperature, with any kind of Peruvian food. **Makes 1 cup**

Note: Onions that have been sliced, then left to stand around for an interminable length of time develop an unpleasant aroma and taste. Therefore, it is suggested that *Zarza* be served immediately after it is prepared.

Zarza (All Peru)

RED ONION SALSA

This ensalada de la mesa (everyday table condiment) is a common favorite throughout the country of Peru. It is best made right before serving and does not keep its freshness for even one day if stored.

- 1   **pound red onions**
- ¼   **cup fresh lime juice**
- ½   **teaspoon salt**

Peel the onions and cut in half. Turn the halves on their sides and slice thin. In a bowl toss the onions with the lime juice and salt.

Serve cool or at room temperature. **Makes about 1 cup**

Zarza (Chincha)

RED ONION AND TOMATO SIDE DISH

- 1   **red onion, sliced thin (½ cup)**
- 1   **ripe tomato, cut into small dice**
- 1   **teaspoon salt, or to taste**
- ⅛   **teaspoon pepper**
-      **Juice of 1 lemon**

Mix all the ingredients together.

Serve either chilled or at room temperature, with *chicharrónes*. **Makes about ¾ cup**

Salsa Criolla (Iquitos)

EVERYDAY TABLE CONDIMENT

An accompaniment to everyday food.

- 2   medium red onions, sliced thin (1 cup)
- 3   tablespoons fresh lime juice
- ½   teaspoon chopped seeded fresh *aji amarillo* (yellow Peruvian chili, see Glossary), or more to taste
- ⅛   teaspoon cumin
- ⅛   teaspoon pepper
- 1   tablespoon chopped fresh cilantro
- ½   teaspoon salt

Mix all the ingredients together.

Serve at room temperature or cold. **Makes about 1¼ cups**

Salsa de Ceballa Picada (Iquitos)

CHOPPED ONION CONDIMENT DYNAMITE STYLE

This easy-to-assemble side dish that is served with any sort of Amazonian food is a regional condiment of the jungle people. This should not imply that the aborigine peoples one sees coming into Iquitos to sell their wares are the only ones who eat it. This very hot condiment should be treated judiciously.

Included in this salsa is the aji charapa, a wild, very hot round cherry-sized chili found near Iquitos. The ones I saw (and tasted!) in a salad were yellow balls of dynamite.

- 2   small *aji charapa* (see Glossary) or other similarly hot chilies
- 1   large red onion, chopped not too fine (1 cup)
- 3   tablespoons fresh lime juice
- 1   teaspoon salt

Crush the chilies slightly to release their sting. Then combine all the ingredients together in a medium bowl. Let stand 30 minutes before using.

Serve as a side dish, with Juane (see Index). **Makes about 1 1/4 cups**

Salta Piquante (Chincha)

HOT SAUCE CONDIMENT

Yellow aji chili powder provides the paramount jolt in this well-seasoned hot table sauce. Heat alone, though, is an inadequate characteristic for a condiment, and this one is enhanced by garlic, cilantro, vinegar, and onion, among other ingredients. Spicy chili heat should not be an affliction to be tolerated but a culinary adjunct, added according to personal preference.

1	teaspoon corn oil
1	large onion, chopped
2	cloves garlic, sliced
3	teaspoon dried yellow *aji* chili powder (see **Glossary**)
8	sprigs fresh cilantro, trim ends, chopped
½	teaspoon salt
⅛	teaspoon pepper
6	soda crackers (see **Note**)
1	teaspoon distilled white or cider vinegar
2	teaspoons olive oil
½	cup water

1. Heat the corn oil in a skillet. Add the onion and garlic and stir-fry over low heat for 2 minutes. Cool.

2. Transfer the onion mixture to a blender or food processor and add all the remaining ingredients. Process until smooth.

Serve at room temperature, with any Peruvian food, but it is especially

recommended with meat dishes. Can be refrigerated for 2 days only.
Makes about 1½ cups

Note: Soda crackers (saltines) are sometimes used as a thickener in Peruvian cooking.

Aguadito – Salsa de Cebolla (Puno)

COOKED ONION SALAD, A SIDE DISH

This is a side dish that is designed to enhance the taste and add dimension to the entrée being served, be it meat or fish.

I	**tablespoon corn oil**
I	**pound onions, halved and cut into long slices**
½	**cup chopped tomato**
I	**sweet red pepper, chopped coarse (½ cup)**
¼	**teaspoon cumin**
¼	**teaspoon pepper**
I	**teaspoon salt, or to taste**

Heat the oil in a skillet large enough to contain all the vegetables. Add the onions and stir-fry over low heat for 1 minute. Add the tomato and red pepper and stir-fry for 2 minutes. Add the cumin, pepper, and salt and continue to stir-fry for 2 minutes as some liquid accumulates.

Serve warm, about 2 generous tablespoons sprinkled over any kind of altiplano meat or fish dishes from Puno. **Serves 4 to 6**

Uchucuta/Aji Picante (Cuzco)

GROUND NUT CONDIMENT

*Here is an unusual and effective table condiment with some spice heat to it.
Brazil nuts are grown in the Amazon and can be seen for sale in the public
markets. Uchucuta is the name of this condiment in an Incan dialect.*

8	**Brazil nuts or 2 tablespoons dry roasted peanuts or both**
½	**cup fresh cilantro leaves and young steams**
1	**tablespoon chopped flat-leaf parsley**
½	**teaspoon salt**
1	**fresh *aji amarillo* (yellow Peruvian chili, see Glossary), seeded and sliced**
¼	**cup water**

In a food processor grind the nuts until broken into coarse pieces. Add
all the remaining ingredients and process to a smooth paste.

Serve with any Peruvian food, but especially with the dishes from
Cuzco. **Makes ¾ cup**

Batido de Rocotos (Arequipa)

MASHED ROCOTOS WITH GARLIC

A rocoto *is a semi-hot chili, the size of small supermarket red and green pepper. Seeded and with the veins removed, it still retains a mild spice. When one hears about* rocotos *in the northern cities of Peru, they are always linked with the city of Arequipa, where they are used frequently in several ways. Here is a spicy table condiment that can be served with any Peruvian food.*

5	whole *rocotos* (about 1 pound, see Note)
1	whole head of garlic
1	medium ripe tomato, peeled and chopped fine (½ cup)
½	teaspoon salt, or more to taste

1. Roast the *rocotos* and garlic in a preheated 400 degree oven until soft. The *rocotos* will take less time, since they are a soft vegetable, about 15 to 20 minutes. The garlic may take about ½ hour to become soft to the touch.

2. Cool and peel the *rocotos* and garlic. In a bowl mash them well, then add the tomato and salt, whipping them together briskly with a fork.

Serve at room temperature, as a table condiment with meat and fish dishes. **Serves 6 to 8**

Note: Rocotos are not available unless one finds them from a very specialized grower in the United States. However, try substituting sweet red or green peppers (red is better) and add 1 fresh *aji amarillo* (see Glossary), seeded and chopped, when you stir in the tomato and salt.

Cauche de Queso (Arequipa)

CHEESE SAUCE FROM A PICANTERIA

Evaporated milk holds an important place in the cooking of Arequipa as well as other cities in Peru. Cans of Dutch milk are seen everywhere and add a rich thickness to sauces, soups, and stews. This sauce is used over potatoes, Peruvian style, and by stretching the idea a little farther it could also be served over broccoli, green peas, or your favorite cooked vegetable.

1	tablespoon corn oil
3	small onions, quartered (1 pound)
1½	pounds (6) small potatoes, cooked in their skin, peeled, and left whole or cut into ½-inch-thick slices
1½	cups evaporated milk
½	pound chopped *queso fresco* (see Glossary) or crumbled Feta
1	teaspoon salt, or to taste
¼	teaspoon pepper
1	tablespoon *huacatay* (see Glossary)
¼	teaspoon turmeric

1. Heat the oil in a skillet. Add the onion quarters and stir-fry over low heat for 1 minute. Add the potatoes and stir to coat.

2. Add the milk, cheese, salt, pepper, *huacatay*, and turmeric and shake the pan vigorously to melt the cheese and mix the ingredients together. Cook over low heat for 3 to 5 minutes.

Serve hot, 1 potato per person. **Serves 6**

Salsa con Tamarindo (Callao)

TAMARIND SAUCE WITH PINEAPPLE

*How to explain the oddity of a tamarind sauce that contains
no natural tamarind paste in it at all?*

*The sauce, (tamarind or not) is sweet and has a definite Chinese
(Chifa) influence. It is customarily served with three different items—pork,
breast of chicken, or fish, all of them cooked separately.*

8	canned pineapple cubes
1	carrot, sliced thin diagonally (¾ cup)
3	tablespoons ketchup
3	tablespoons red wine vinegar
1	to 2 tablespoons sugar, or to taste
1	teaspoon soy sauce
⅛	teaspoon ground cinnamon
3	scallions, sliced thin diagonally
½	sweet red pepper, cut into long and thin slices (½ cup)
18	snow peas
1	tablespoon cornstarch, dissolved in 3 tablespoons cold water

1. Put the pineapple, carrot, ketchup, vinegar, sugar, soy sauce,
cinnamon in a pan and simmer over low heat for 2 minutes. Add the
scallions, red pepper, and enough of the cornstarch mixture to lightly
thicken the sauce. Simmer for 2 more minutes to integrate all the
flavors and fold in the snow peas.

Serve warm, with either pork, chicken, or fish. **Makes about 2 cups**

Escribano (Arequipa)

SALAD SIDE DISH

Potatoes turn up everywhere in Peruvian cooking. They are the filler on the table, since bread is not automatically served, except perhaps for breakfast. This simple combination makes an attractive adjunct to a meal.

1	**medium potato**
1	**medium tomato, peeled and cut into 1/4-inch dice**
2	**teaspoons red wine vinegar**
1	**teaspoon corn or olive oil**
¼	**teaspoon pepper**
⅛	**teaspoon salt**
½	**teaspoon chopped parsley**

1. Cook the potato in its skin in boiling water until soft. Drain. Cool, peel, and cut in half.

2. In a bowl gently mix the potato with the remaining ingredients.

Serve as a side dish with Arequipa foods. **Serves 2**

Ensalada Mixta (Lambayeque)

ASSORTED MIXED VEGETABLE SALAD

*I went to the small but complete public market with Isabel,
the mother of thirteen children of all ages, to buy enough ingredients for an
all-day cooking extravaganza in her simple home. Four live pigeons, duck,
corn oil, evaporated milk, fresh cheese, onion, garlic, eggs, potatoes—the list
was long as we wandered around the open-air town market. Then we
went home in a bicycle taxi and started to cook.*

*Peruvians do not eat many vegetables, which seem to be an adjunct
rather than an important feature of their cooking. This mixed salad,
though simple, has variety and was to be served with duck.*

2	pounds beets, cooked and cut into ½-inch cubes
1	pound potato, cooked, peeled, and cut into ½-inch cubes
2	medium carrots, cooked and cut into ½-inch cubes (1 cup)
1	cup fresh or frozen green peas, blanched in hot water and drained
1	small onion, cut into small dice (⅓ cup)
½	teaspoon salt
1	tablespoon olive or corn oil
1	tablespoon distilled white vinegar
⅛	teaspoon pepper

1. In a bowl combine all the ingredients and toss.

Serve at room temperature. **Serves 6 to 8**

Soltero de Queso Zarza (Arequipa)

FRESH CHEESE SALAD SIDE DISH

A zarza is a typical criolla *salad, and there are many different versions that can accompany a meal. A* picanteria *where I dined frequently served a number of these side dishes, some with unconventional ingredients. You had to really read the menu because some of the zarzas, all nicely preserved in sliced julienne strips, included cow's lips, stomach, and testicles. (It was a matter of textures and flavors.) The following recipe, a favorite in Arequipa, is prepared with mozzarella cheese.*

½	**pound mozzarella or more to taste, cut into ½-inch pieces**
1	**medium onion, cut into small dice (½ cup)**
2	**hard-boiled eggs, peeled and cubed**
1	**ripe medium tomato, cut into ½-inch cubes (½ cup)**
1	**tablespoon chopped parsley**
½	**teaspoon salt, or to taste**
⅛	**teaspoon pepper**
2	**teaspoons white wine vinegar**
2	**teaspoons fresh lime juice**

In a bowl combine all the ingredients together, toss several times.

Serve with broiled white or sweet potatoes, whole or sliced. **Serves 6 to 8 as an appetizer**

Salpicon (Arequipa)

SALAD SIDE DISH WITH BEEF

Usually one hears the word zarza *used in reference to a salad side dish. This one includes boiled beef, frequently leftover beef, but one can substitute roasted or boiled chicken.*

3	to 4 cups shredded lettuce
1	medium onion, cut into small dice (⅓ cup)
1	large ripe tomato, cut into small dice (¾ cup)
4	sprigs flat-leaf parsley, chopped
1	sprig fresh cilantro, chopped
1	cup diced boiled beef
½	teaspoon salt
⅛	teaspoon pepper
¼	teaspoon sugar
2	tablespoons red wine vinegar or more, to taste
2	teaspoons olive oil

In a bowl toss all the ingredients together thoroughly.

Serve at room temperature as an appetizer with bread. **Serves 6**

Zarza de Patitas de Chancho (Arequipa)

PIG'S FEET SALAD SIDE DISH

A zarza is usually a starter that whets the appetite for the bigger game that is expected in the entrée. Simple to prepare and enticing, Patitas are a long-time favorite in Latin America.

3	pig's feet, halved lengthwise
½	teaspoon plus 1 teaspoon salt
2	tablespoons white wine vinegar
¼	teaspoon pepper
1	tablespoon corn oil
2	medium onions, sliced thin (about 1 cup)
1	medium tomato, peeled and sliced thin (½ cup)
1	tablespoon chopped parsley

1. Cook the pig's feet in boiling water until soft, about 1 hour. Drain, cool completely, and remove the small bones. Then slice the gelatinous meat into julienne strips.

2. Put the slices in a bowl of warm water and add the ½ teaspoon salt. Soak for 5 minutes. Drain.

3. Return the strips to the bowl and add the vinegar, pepper, and oil. Stir to combine. Add the onions, tomato, parsley, and the 1 teaspoon salt. Toss well. Serve or cover and refrigerate.

Serve at room temperature or cold. **Serves 6 to 8**

Patita de Chancho en Fiambre (Trujillo)

PIG'S FEET IN VINEGAR SAUCE

This is an old-time recipe, very criolla *style, when home cooks entered the kitchens of Peru early in the morning and remained there most of the day preparing for large family meals. Patita is considered an appetizer, one that is substantially assisted by the yuca that serves as filler.*

2	pound pig's feet, halved lengthwise
8	cups (2 quarts) water
2½	teaspoons salt
I	pound onions, peeled, cut into thin slices, and rinsed in cold water
2	to 3 tablespoons distilled white vinegar, to taste
⅛	teaspoon pepper
2	tablespoons corn oil
I	teaspoon dried yellow *aji* chili powder (see Glossary)
½	teaspoon turmeric
I	teaspoon dried oregano
	Lettuce leaves
I	pound yuca (see Glossary), peeled, cut into index-finger-sized-pieces, and cooked, for serving

1. Cook the pig's feet in the water with 2 teaspoons of the salt over moderate heat for 1 hour, or more, until tender. Drain, reserving ½ cup broth. Let the pig's feet cool, cover, and refrigerate.

2. In a large bowl combine the onions, vinegar, remaining ½ teaspoon salt, and pepper.

3. In a skillet heat the oil and fry the chili powder over low heat for 2 minutes. Add the onion mixture, turmeric, and oregano and mix well. Add the ½ cup reserved broth, cover the skillet, and cook for 2 minutes. Taste and adjust the salt. Refrigerate the sauce until ready to dine.

To serve, line a platter with the lettuce. Place the pig's feet in the center and arrange the yuca around the meat. Pour the vinegar sauce over the pig's feet.

Serve cold. Eat with your fingers. **Serves 6**

Ensalada de Pulpo (Chincha)
OCTOPUS SALAD

Seafood is paramount in the life of the people of Chincha living,
as they do, near the remarkable coastline of Peru, with its equally astonishing
seafood industry. Salads are part of what is prepared there and contain
seafood, such as octopus. A young octopus does not require a lot of cooking.
The older and larger they are, the tougher they become. A young octopus of
about two pounds should be tender and tasty.

1	**small young octopus, about 2 pounds, well rinsed in cold water**
1	**medium onion, cut into thin slices (1 cup)**
	Juice of 1 or 2 green limes, to taste
½	**teaspoon salt**
⅛	**teaspoon pepper**
1	**ripe medium tomato, chopped (¾ cup)**
5	**sprigs cilantro, chopped fine**
½	**cup diced cooked carrot (¼-inch pieces)**
1	**potato, cooked and cut into ½-inch cubes (1 cup)**
½	**cup green peas, lightly cooked**
1	**tablespoon olive oil**
	Lettuce leaves

1. Cook the whole octopus in water to cover for about 30 minutes to tenderize. (It should be only slightly firm.) Drain. Cool, then remove

and discard the head and mouth. Rinse well in cold water. Cut the body and tentacles into thin round slices.

2. Rinse the onion slices in cold water and drain well. In a bowl combine the onion slices with the lime juice, salt, and pepper and toss. Now add the tomato, cilantro, carrot, potato, green peas, and olive oil. Toss to mix well. Cover and refrigerate until chilled.

To serve, line a serving bowl or platter with the lettuce leaves and top with the salad.

Serve cool. **Serves 6 to 8**

⁓⁓⁓ VEGETABLE DISHES ⁓⁓⁓

Kapche 1 (Cuzco)

FAVA BEANS, MUSHROOMS, AND CHINESE MELANGE

This inventive preparation is a Spanish colonial dish from the Seventeenth and Eighteenth Centuries and is popular in Cuzco, which has its own historical connection with the Spanish Conquest.

2	tablespoons corn oil
1	large onion, chopped (1 cup)
3	cloves garlic, ground to a paste with 2 tablespoons water
2	teaspoons salt, or to taste
¼	teaspoon cumin
¼	teaspoon pepper
1	cup hot water
1	pound shelled fresh fava beans
1	pound mushrooms, wiped clean and halves
1	cup cubed *queso fresco* (see Glossary) or Feta cheese
1	cup milk
2	eggs, beaten
1	tablespoon chopped parsley

1. Heat the oil in a large pan. Add the onion and garlic and stir-fry over high heat for 2 minutes. Add the salt, cumin, and pepper and toss briefly to combine.

2. Add the hot water and bring to a boil. Add the fava beans and mushrooms and simmer until tender, several minutes. Add the cheese and the milk and simmer for 2 or 3 minutes more.

3. Stir in the eggs, sprinkle the parsley over all, and cover the pan. Remove the pan from the heat and let stand for 5 minutes before serving.

Serve warm, with rice. **Serves 8**

Kapche de Hongos 2 (Cuzco)

WILD MUSHROOM MÉLANGE

*During the rainy season—November, December, and January—wild
mushrooms are gathered in the Andean hills near Cuzco. At an altitude of
about 10,000 feet or more, where it is treeless, empty, and frigid, the
mushrooms thrive and so do the famous potatoes of Peru.*

2	tablespoons corn oil
1	medium onion, chopped (½ cup)
4	cloves garlic, crushed
½	teaspoon dried oregano
¼	teaspoon turmeric
5	cups water
2	teaspoons salt, or to taste
10	small potatoes, about 1½ inches diameter, peeled
2	pounds fresh wild mushrooms, such as shiitake or portobellos, cleaned and cut into 2-inch slices
1	cup chopped *queso fresco* (see Glossary) or Feta cheese
2	eggs, beaten
1	cup evaporated milk (preferred) or fresh milk
1	tablespoon *huacatay* (see Glossary)

1. Heat the oil in a pan. Add the onion, garlic, oregano, and turmeric
and stir-fry over low heat for 2 minutes. Add the water and salt and
bring to a boil.

2. Add the potatoes and cook until soft, about 20 minutes. Add the
mushrooms. In a bowl mix together the cheese and eggs and add to the
potato mixture. Stir in the milk and *huacatay* until combined and
simmer for 5 minutes.

Serve hot, in bowls. **Serves 8 to 10**

Espesado de Garbanzos (Trujillo)

PURÉE OF GARBANZOS

*This purée is vegetarian and can be served as an accompaniment
with stuffed vegetables or meat dishes.*

½	**pound dried garbanzos (chick peas)**
1½	**cups water**
2	**tablespoons corn oil**
2	**tablespoons chopped onion**
2	**cloves garlic, chopped**
½	**teaspoon salt, or to taste**

1. Soak the garbanzos in water overnight, 8 to 10 hours. Drain. In a
food processor process the soaked (but not cooked) garbanzos with
1½ cups water until puréed.

2. Heat the oil in a pan or skillet. Add the onion and garlic and stir-fry
over low heat until the onion changes color, about 2 minutes. Add the
salt and garbanzo purée and stir-fry about 15 minutes, still over low
heat. If the mixture appears too dry, add several tablespoons water to
retain the purée consistency. Adjust the salt.

Serve warm. **Serves 8 as a side dish**

Peske de Quinoa (Puno)

PURÉE OF QUINOA

*It was All Saint's Day (Todos Los Santos) and the public market in Puno
was filling up with throngs of people, all buying the many varieties of fruit
that had been brought in from warmer climates—bananas, the largest and
sweetest kiwis, mangoes, grapes, apples, oranges, among others.*

*In the food kiosks, a good-natured cook was preparing this purée
of quinoa for the midday lunch crowd.*

3	cups water
2	cups quinoa (see Glossary), well rinsed, soaked in water 1 hour and drained (see Note)
1	teaspoon salt, or to taste
½	cup mozzarella cheese, cut into small cubes
1	cup milk

1. Bring the water to a boil in a pan, add the soaked quinoa, and
simmer over low heat for 30 minutes, which will soften it
considerably. Transfer to a food processor and purée. Transfer the
purée to a bowl, add the salt, and fold in the cheese and milk. Mix well.

Serve hot, with any of the meat dishes from Puno. **Serves 6**

Note: Before cooking it, I like to soak quinoa in water to cover for 1 hour. The
cooks of Puno do not do this; they simply cook it until it is soft, saying that the
cooking doesn't take long.

Papa a la Huancaina Estilo Chiclayano (Chiclayo)

POTATO AND FRESH CHEESE APPETIZER CHICLAYO STYLE

A very long title for one of the most popular and delicious foods in Peru.
This version differs from the original in the high mountain city of Huancayo,
where the cooked potatoes are sliced lengthwise. In Chiclayo, the potatoes
are mashed and shaped into balls as below.

½	pound sliced *queso fresco* (see Glossary) or Feta cheese
¾	cup evaporated milk or, if preferred, fresh milk
2	teaspoons dried yellow *aji* chili powder (see Glossary)
2	teaspoons corn oil
2	pounds potatoes, cooked until soft in the skins
½	teaspoon salt
⅛	teaspoon pepper
8	lettuce leaves
2	hard-boiled eggs, peeled and quartered
8	black olives, pitted

1. Put the cheese, milk, chili powder, and oil in a blender and process until creamy.

2. Peel the potatoes, then mash until smooth. Add the salt and pepper and mix well. Form slightly flattened balls, about 2½ inches in diameter, with the mashed potatoes.

Place 1 lettuce leaf on the plate. Top with 1 mashed potato ball. Pour ¼ cup cheese sauce over the potato and garnish with 1 egg quarter and an olive.

Serve at room temperature. **Serves 8 as an appetizer**

Papa de la Huancaina (Lima)

POTATOES IN CHEESE SAUCE

*The sauce is pale yellow in color thanks to the medium-hot aji chili.
Depending upon what is available, either fresh or dried powder can be used.
The cheese recommended is queso fresco (also called fresh cheese), which
can be reduced in a blender to a smooth consistency.*

*The place of origin in Peru of this universally appreciated, yet simple dish is the
mountain town of Huancayo, a few hours from Lima. Each region or even city
has a certain twist to the recipe, however, which is a personal preference of the
cook. No matter what, it is served everywhere and when in doubt as to what to
have for lunch, the choice is frequently Papa a la Huancaina.*

2	**pounds potatoes**
3	**fresh *aji amarillo* (yellow Peruvian chili, see Glossary), seeded and chopped, or 3 teaspoons dried yellow *aji* chili powder**
2	**soda crackers, crushed fine**
I	**cup evaporated milk**
I	**teaspoon salt, or to taste**
½	**cup chopped *queso fresco* (see Glossary) or Feta cheese**
6	**lettuce leaves**
2	**hard-boiled eggs, peeled and quartered**
6	**black olives, pitted**

1. Cook the potatoes in boiling water until soft but still with a certain firmness. Cool, peel, and set aside.

2. Put the *aji*, crackers, milk, salt, and cheese in a blender and process until smooth.

3. Slice the potatoes lengthwise about ¼ inch thick or a bit thicker.

To serve, line a large platter with the lettuce leaves and cover with the potato slices. Pour the sauce over the potatoes and garnish with the quartered eggs and olives.

Note: The dish may also be served on individual salad plates equally divided.

Serve at room temperature. **Serves 6 as an appetizer**

Papa a la Diabla (Callao)
DEVILLED POTATOES WITH YELLOW AJI CHILI

This unusual home-cooked recipe of a friend's grandmother uses fresh yellow aji, queso fresco (fresh cheese), evaporated milk, and a lot of potatoes. All of these are milestones on the road to the national cooking of Peru. An authentic family-style dish, vegetarian and original.

2	pounds potatoes (4 or 5)
¼	cup olive oil
2	fresh or canned whole *aji amarillo* (see Note)
4	whole cloves garlic
2	pounds onions, chopped fine (3 cups)
¼	teaspoon turmeric
⅛	teaspoon pepper
I	cup chopped *queso fresco* (see Glossary) or domestic or imported Feta cheese
I	cup evaporated milk
	Lettuce leaves
4	hard-boiled eggs, peeled and halved
8	black olives
	Sweet red pepper, cut into long julienne strips

1. Cook the potatoes in the skins until tender. Drain, cool, peel, and slice lengthwise about ½ inch thick. Set aside.

2. Heat the oil in a large skillet. Add the *aji* and garlic and brown them lightly for 2 minutes. Remove and in a food processor process them to a purée with 2 tablespoons water.

3. Add the onion to the skillet with the turmeric and pepper and stir-fry over low heat until the onion turns yellow. Stir in the *aji*/garlic purée.

4. In the food processor blend the cheese and the milk together until smooth. Add to onion mixture and simmer over low heat for 3 minutes.

To serve, line a large serving platter with the lettuce leaves. Top with the sliced potatoes. Pour the cream sauce over the potatoes. Garnish the potatoes with the eggs, olives, and red pepper strips.

Serve at room temperature. **Serves 8 as an appetizer**

Note: Whole yellow *aji*, fresh or canned, may not always be available. In that case, substitute the dried *aji* chili powder; 1 teaspoon powder equals 1 whole fresh or canned yellow *aji*. For more information on *ajis*, see the Glossary.

Pastel de Papa (Arequipa)
POTATO PIE

*Arequipa is a beautiful city that stands in the shadow of
several extinct volcanoes. It is known for its good cooks and preoccupation
with good dining. Dairy products, butter, and cheese are manufactured
here and sold in other parts of the country.*

5	**pounds potatoes**
8	**cups (2 quarts) water**
5	**eggs**
I	**cup evaporated milk or fresh milk**
I	**cup hot water**
2	**teaspoons salt**
¼	**teaspoon pepper**
2	**teaspoons anise seeds**
2	**tablespoons butter**
½	**pound mozzarella cheese, cut into 3-inch-long slices**

1. Bring the 8 cups of water to a boil. Meanwhile, peel the potatoes and slice them into medium-thick rounds. Add the potato slices to the water and bring to a boil again. Drain immediately. Set aside.

2. Beat 3 of the eggs with the milk, hot water, salt, pepper, and anise seeds. Set aside.

3. Rub a large Pyrex dish or other baking dish with the butter. Arrange the potato slices in layers in the dish. Cover with the cheese slices. Pour the milk mixture over the ingredients. Beat the remaining 2 eggs well and pour over the top. Bake in a preheated 325 degree oven for 45 minutes, or until the top is brown.

Serve warm. **Serves 8**

Plato Huanchaquero (Huanchaco)

POTATOES AND SEAWEED, A VEGETARIAN DISH

This is an appetizer plate from the Huanchaco, where fresh seaweed is harvested by divers off the extensive beach of this resort a few minutes' drive from Trujillo.
The seaweed (yuyo) is sold, thinly sliced, in a small marketplace just off the beach. Potatoes are everywhere in Peru. This typical recipe is a logical outcome of how people live off the land in a vegetarian way in Huanchaco.

- 1   tablespoon corn or olive oil
- 2   tablespoons chopped onion
- 1   clove garlic, chopped fine
- 1   teaspoon paprika (for color)
- ¼   teaspoon salt
- 2   medium potatoes, peeled, cooked, and quartered (about 1 cup)
- 1   cup yuyo (fresh seaweed, the thin and long strands, see Glossary)

Sauces, Salads, and Vegetable Dishes ~ 229

Heat the oil in a skillet. Add the onion, garlic, paprika, and salt and stir-fry over moderate heat for 1 minute. Add the potatoes and yuyo and stir-fry for 3 minutes until heated through.

Serve warm. **Serves 4 as an appetizer**

Tacu-Tacu (Trujillo)

BEANS AND RICE

This vegetarian combination is usually (but does not have to be) served with steak or liver dishes. It can stand on its own since Peruvian cooks prepare the rice here with 2 teaspoons corn oil, 1 clove garlic, crushed, and ½ teaspoon salt and they do this automatically. With this in mind, do not oversalt the dish. I did not prepare the rice that way.

- ½ teaspoon salt
- 1 cup dried white beans, soaked in water to cover overnight and drained
- 4 cups (1 quart) water
- 1½ cups rice, well rinsed, soaked in water to cover ½ hour, and drained
- 2 teaspoons finely chopped cilantro
- 1 clove garlic, chopped fine

1. Cook the beans in the 4 cups water until soft, about 1 hour. Drain.

2. Meanwhile, cook the rice with the salt in the conventional manner.

3. Mix the rice and beans together with the cilantro and garlic.

Serve warm, with steak or liver dishes. **Serves 6**

Tallarines al Horno (Cuzco)

BAKED SPAGHETTI

Not all the food of Peru has an antique antecedent. Here is a modern vegetarian pasta preparation that is popular in Cuzco. There are no exotic spices and seasonings but nevertheless it has a Peruvian slant.

2	pounds dried spaghetti, broken in half
2½	teaspoons salt
3	tablespoons corn oil
2	medium onions, chopped (1 cup)
2	cups ripe tomatoes, peeled and chopped
½	pound mozzarella cheese, cubed
2	hard-boiled eggs, peeled and sliced
½	cup pitted black olives, halved
2	eggs, beaten

1. Bring a large pot of water to a boil. Add the spaghetti and 2 teaspoons salt and cook for about 8 minutes, until *al dente*. Drain, and set aside.

2. Heat 2 tablespoons of the oil in a skillet. Add the onions and tomatoes, season with the ½ teaspoon salt, and stir-fry over low heat for 5 minutes.

3. Rub a 9 x 12-inch Pyrex baking dish with the remaining 1 tablespoon oil. Cover the bottom with half of the spaghetti. Spread the cheese over that and top with onion/tomato mixture. Scatter the hard-boiled egg slices and olives over the vegetables. Top with the remaining spaghetti. Dribble the 2 beaten eggs over the top. Bake in a preheated 350 degree oven until light brown on the top, 15 to 20 minutes.

Serve hot, cut into squares. **Serves 8 to 10**

Tallarines en Salsa Verde (Callao)

SPAGHETTI IN GREEN SAUCE

Here is one of the most popular Italian-inspired dishes, but done in the Peruvian style of cooking. The arrival of the Italians in the mid-Nineteenth Century resulted in a display of their culture and the beginning of the grape/wine industry in Ica. After a time their pasta dishes were adopted by the general public and have now become Peruvian by osmosis. This is one of my favorite dishes.

2	pounds dried spaghetti (#9)
¼	cup walnuts
½	pound chopped *queso fresco* (see Glossary) or Feta cheese
1½	cups fresh basil leaves (stemmed), chopped
3	cups spinach leaves only (stemmed), chopped
½	cup evaporated milk
2	cloves garlic, sliced
1	tablespoon chopped red onion
1	teaspoon salt
2	tablespoons grated Parmesan cheese
¼	cup green string beans, cut into 1-inch pieces, cooked *al dente*

1. In a large pot cook the spaghetti in boiling water about 1 minute, until *al dente*. Drain, rinse well with cold water, and drain again. Set aside.

2. In a food processor blend the following ingredients into a smooth creamy sauce. First, the walnuts, then add the cheese, basil, spinach, milk, garlic, onion, salt, and the 2 tablespoons olive oil.

3. Heat the 2 teaspoons olive oil in a skillet. Add the sauce and warm slowly over low heat for about 3 minutes.

4. In a large serving bowl toss the spaghetti and beans with the sauce to integrate the textures and flavors. Sprinkle with the Parmesan cheese.

Serve warm, with French fries, fried steak, or fish fillets. **Serves 8**

Tempura de Vegetales (Peruvian/Japanese)

FRIED VEGETABLE DUMPLINGS

These dumplings are best eaten hot, right after they have emerged from the oil and been drained on paper towels. Tempura, as we know from restaurants, is slices of pieces of vegetables enrobed in a batter and deep fried. Dumplings are a tasty and different method for this cross-cultural cooking.

12	large eggs, beaten
1	cup flour
2	teaspoons salt, or to taste
1	cup diced carrot (¼ inch pieces)
2	cups chopped lettuce
1	cup fresh or frozen green peas
1	cup thinly sliced scallion
	Corn oil for deep frying, about 2 to 3 cups

THE SAUCE

½	cup soy sauce (Chinese or Japanese)
½	teaspoon finely chopped ginger
½	teaspoon fresh lime juice

1. Stir the eggs and flour together into a smooth batter in a large bowl. Add the salt and fold in all the vegetables.

2. Heat the oil in a wok or large skillet over high heat. Lower the heat to moderate. Measure heaping tablespoons of the vegetable batter and drop them into the oil. Deep-fry for 5 minutes, until lightly browned all over. Remove and drain briefly on paper towels.

3. Meanwhile, make the sauce: Mix the ingredients together well. Serve at room temperature.

Serve hot, with individual bowls of the dipping sauce as an appetizer, with drinks or as a meal with rice.

Purée de Zapallo (Lambayeque)
PURÉE OF ZAPALLO

One of the astonishing sights in the public markets of Peru is the enormous zapallo *(a squash), each one of which could be a candidate for a prize at a New England autumn fair. The vendors cut it into orange/gold slices and sell it by the piece.*

2	pounds *zapallo* (see Glossary) or butternut squash, peeled and cut into cubes
2	cups water
1	teaspoon salt, or to taste
1	tablespoon butter
1	tablespoon finely chopped onion
2	tablespoons finely chopped ripe tomato
2	tablespoons milk
⅛	teaspoon pepper

1. In a medium pan cook the squash in the water with ½ of the teaspoon salt until soft, about 15 minutes. Drain, mash and return to the pan.

2. Heat the butter in a pan or skillet. Add the onion and tomato, and stir-fry over low heat for 2 minutes. Add to the mashed squash with the milk, the remaining ½ teaspoon salt, and pepper. Mix well over low heat for 5 minutes, reducing the mixture to a smooth purée.

Serve warm. **Serves 6**

Aji de Calabaza (Arequipa)
ZAPALLO STEW WITH AJI CHILI

Zapallo is the giant calabash family of squash that is found all over Peru. Some are of astonishing size. This stew, which is vegetarian, has a rich combination of ingredients that is most satisfying.

3	cloves garlic, sliced
1	tablespoon dried yellow *aji* chili powder (see Glossary)
¼	teaspoon turmeric
¼	teaspoon cumin
¼	cup water
2	tablespoons corn oil
5	pounds *zapallo* (see Glossary) or butternut squash, peeled, cut into long thin slices, and quartered
1	large onion, coarsely sliced (1 cup)
½	cup shelled fresh fava beans
1	pound potato, peeled and cut into little-finger-sized pieces
¼	cup fresh or frozen corn kernels
1	cup small cubes *queso fresco* (see Glossary) or Feta cheese
1	teaspoon *huacatay* (see Glossary)
2	teaspoons salt, or to taste
½	cup evaporated milk mixed with ½ cup water

1. In a food processor process the garlic, chili powder, turmeric, and cumin with ¼ cup water to a paste.

2. Heat the oil in a large pan. Add the seasoning paste and stir-fry it over low heat for 2 minutes.

3. In separate pans of boiling water, blanch the squash, onion, fava beans, and potato for ½ minute. Drain well. Add all the vegetables to the pan with the corn, cheese, *huacatay*, and salt.

4. Now add the milk/water and simmer over low heat for about 10 to 15 minutes, stirring now and then. All the vegetables should be soft and moist and the natural flavors blended.

Serve warm, with rice. **Serves 8 or more**

su hijo don fº guaynacatura don jusscopanicra

caes k reyno   don

DESSERTS AND BEVERAGES

Peruvian desserts run the gamut from Mazamorra Morada (page 246), a beautiful concoction prepared with the pre-Hispanic purple corn but reputed to have been invented in Lima, to Budin (page 245), the richly infused bread pudding that could only have come from Europe to a Volteada Crema caramel custards that would satisfy even the most jaded sweet tooth.

Although the culinary influence is predominantly (when it comes to desserts) from the time of the Conquista, the creole hand has modified what appeared from overseas and through metamorphosis made it Peruvian. (This could also apply to other categories of the cuisine.) Not everything sprang with the wave of a magic wand. Ways of cooking developed over the centuries and were then codified into national recipes that can be identified by the cooks throughout Peru.

Desserts are Peruvian home cooking at their best and cannot be faulted for their idiosyncratic combinations. The phrase "you are what you eat" has never been better applied.

Leche Asada (Arequipa)
BAKED CUSTARD

Step into almost any snack or coffee shop and you will see individual Pyrex cups of this custard. One finds it all over the country. The custard is smooth, cooling, and aromatic.

1	**cup evaporated milk**
4	**eggs**
½	**cup sugar**
½	**teaspoon ground cinnamon**
½	**teaspoon vanilla**

1. In a large bowl beat the milk and eggs together for a minute. Now add all the remaining ingredients and mix well.

2. Half-fill 10 individual heatproof custard cups (or one large baking dish). Put the cups (or dish) in a large, low-sided baking pan and add enough water to the baking pan to come halfway up the sides of the cups. Bake in a preheated 400 degree oven for 1 hour. The custards should be firm. Now run the cups under the broiler to brown the tops lightly. Refrigerate.

Serve cold. **Makes 10 cups**

Manjar Blanco (Lambayeque)
AROMATIC MILK CUSTARD

A simple sweet custard with cinnamon and clove. A family favorite.

4	**cups (1 quart) evaporated milk or fresh milk**
2	**cinnamon stocks, each about 3 inches long**
2	**cups sugar**

2   teaspoons cornstarch dissolved in 2 tablespoons
    cold water

2   whole cloves

1   teaspoon vanilla

1. Bring the milk to a boil in a pan over low heat. Add the cinnamon sticks and stir continuously for about ½ hour. Add the sugar, mix well, and continue to stir until dissolved.

2. Add the cornstarch mixture and cloves. Continue to stir as you add the vanilla. Cook, stirring, until the custard thickens to a relatively firm consistency. Pour into a serving bowl and cool. Then cover and refrigerate.

Serve cold. **Serves 6 or 7**

Mazamorra de Cochina (Chincha)

DIRTY (UNTIDY) CUSTARD

This is a poor man's dessert, prepared from flour, evaporated milk, and a number of aromatic spices, among other things, which proves that one does not need expensive ingredients, especially when there is very little money to spare. This flour-based custard is very good indeed and is an old grandmother's recipe from a Negro family in Chincha.

1½ cups water

1   cinnamon stick, 2 inches long

4   whole cloves

1   cup dark brown sugar

2   cups flour

1   can (12 ounces) evaporated milk

1   tablespoon butter

⅓   cup raisins

1   teaspoon ground cinnamon

1. Mix ½ cup of the water, the cinnamon stick, cloves, and brown sugar together in a pan and simmer over low heat for 10 minutes.

2. Dissolve the flour in the remaining ¾ cup water, stirring briskly until the mixture is smooth, without any lumps. Beat in the evaporated milk, a little at a time, until smooth.

3. Add the flour mixture, a little at a time, to the simmering sugar mixture. Stir in the butter and raisins, always mixing thoroughly to prevent lumps. Simmer for 15 minutes.

4. Pour the mixture into a 9-inch Pyrex dish, square or round, 2 inches high. Sprinkle with the ground cinnamon. Cool to room temperature.

May be served warm or cool. **Serves 6 to 8**

Crema Volteada (All Peru)
CREME CARAMEL PERUVIAN STYLE

A popular dessert in Peru that appears on almost every restaurant menu, whether it be a traditional or modern eatery. Of obvious Spanish origin, the custard is relatively easy to assemble; make the egg base, caramelize the sugar, and bake in a bain-marie for one hour.

8	eggs, beaten
1	can (14 ounces) sweetened condensed milk
1	can (12 ounces) evaporated milk
1	teaspoon vanilla
1	teaspoon dark rum
6	tablespoons sugar
1	teaspoon water

1. Mix the eggs and condensed and evaporated milks together well. Stir in the vanilla and rum.

2. Put the sugar in a heavy skillet and sprinkle the water over it. Melt the sugar over low heat until caramel in color, about 5 to 10 minutes. Quickly pour the hot syrup into a round dish (preferably Pyrex), about 9 inches in diameter and 3 inches deep. Tip the bowl to coat the sides all over with the caramel.

3. Pour the egg mixture into the dish. Place the dish in a baking pan and pour very hot water into the pan to come halfway up the sides of the dish. Bake in a preheated 350 degree oven for 1 hour. The custard should be firm.

4. Remove the dish and cook well, then refrigerate until chilled.

To serve, place a serving platter over the dish and invert the custard onto the platter. (The custard will slip out easily.) Cut in slices like a pie. **Serves 8 or more**

Suspiro de Limena (Lima)

A Lady from Lima Sighs

How to explain the meaning of this quintessential sweet of Spanish origin introduced after the conquest of Peru? It may have been recorded in one of the handwritten ledgers kept by the nuns in convents around the countryside. (I discovered a cache of recipes in a convent but circumstances did not allow me the occasion to translate them.) Needless to say, the lady sighed after tasting this delectable dessert and the name has remained until now.

4	eggs, separated
1	teaspoon vanilla
1	can (12 ounces) sweetened condensed milk, at room temperature
1	can (12 ounces) evaporated milk, at room temperature
2	tablespoons sugar
2	tablespoons port wine
¼	teaspoon ground cinnamon, for serving

1. Beat the egg yolks until lemon colored. Stir in the vanilla.

2. Mix together the condensed and evaporated milks until well blended. Pour into a pan and cook over medium/low heat, stirring continuously with a wooden spoon for about 15 minutes as the mixture slowly thickens and the color darkens. Vigilence is necessary to prevent the milk from scorching. The mixture is ready when the bottom of the pan can be seen as you stir the thickening custard. Stir in the beaten egg yolks and pour the custard into a shallow wide serving dish. Set aside.

3. Beat the egg whites until they reach snow peak stiffness. Set aside. Note that the egg whites are now cooked.

4. Pour the sugar in a small nonstick skillet and add the port wine. Simmer over medium/low heat about 5 to 6 minutes until a syrup forms or until a thread appears when the spoon is lifted from the skillet. Cool slightly, then add to the beaten egg whites in a slow, steady stream, folding it in.

To assemble, drop large spoonfuls of the seasoned egg whites to cover the now-cool custard. Sprinkle the cinnamon over all.

Serve at room temperature or after a brief chilling. The dessert is best eaten the day of preparation. **Serves 6 or 7 as dessert with tea or coffee**

Mousse de Chirmoya (Lima)

CHERIMOYA MOUSSE

The fragrant cherimoya (see Glossary) lends itself easily to being the basis of a mousse. When ripe, but not overly so, the fruit can be pulled apart, the pulp scooped out, and the seeds discarded. Then you beat the custard-like fruit with a fork, which reduces it to a soft mush. Measure the amount of Cherimoya purée and combine it with the other ingredients. Chill well and serve during hot summer days or any other time when the fruit becomes available.

The Peruvians use colapez, which are bundles of transparent gelatin strands made from seaweed. When I lived in Calcutta, my cook there would buy the strands in the market and make lemon, chocolate, or any other flavored mousse with them.

1	**cup cherimoya pulp (see recipe introduction and Glossary)**
½	**teaspoon fresh lemon juice**
1	**package (1 ounce) unflavored gelatin**
¼	**cup cold water**
1	**or 2 tablespoons sugar, to taste**
½	**can (6 ounces) well chilled evaporated milk**
½	**teaspoon vanilla**
	Chocolate sauce, for serving (optional)

1. Mix the cherimoya pulp and lemon juice together to prevent the pulp from discoloring.

2. Sprinkle the gelatin over the cold water and stir to combine. Put the mixture in a small pan and dissolve the gelatin over low heat, which will take less than a minute.

3. In a large bowl beat the sugar and cold milk together until frothy. Add the cherimoya, dissolved gelatin, and vanilla and blend briskly to combine. Pour the mousse mixture into a bowl or rectangular dish and refrigerate for several hours, until set.

To serve, cut into generous portions and top with your favorite chocolate sauce, if desired. **Serves 4 to 6**

Note: Mango Mousse: Cherimoya is a seasonal fruit and not always available when you most want it. Some are grown in Florida and sold in fancy food markets. I have substituted canned mango purée imported from India in 1-pound-14-ounce cans with great success. Simply measure out the amount of mango purée (1 cup) and all the other ingredients, except the lemon juice, which you must omit. Make the mousse as directed, chill, and serve it with the optional chocolate sauce.

Arroz con Leche (Lima)

RICE AND MILK

There are recipes for this traditional dessert all over Peru, and each one claims to be the original. Original or not, they are all good. The dessert is popular. It is even listed on restaurant menus.

8	cups (2 quarts) water
½	cup rice, well rinsed, soaked in water to cover ½ hour, and drained
2	whole cloves
1	cinnamon stick, about 3 inches long
1	cup condensed milk
3	cups evaporated milk
½	cup sugar

1. Put the water into a pan and bring to a boil. Add the rice, cloves, and cinnamon stick and simmer over moderate heat for 7 minutes.

2. Stir in the condensed and evaporated milks and the sugar and cook for 5 minutes, stirring constantly.

Pour the mixture into a bowl and chill well for several hours.

Serve cold. (Some people prefer to have this dessert served at room temperature or even hot.) **Serves 8 generously**

Budin (Chincha)

BREAD PUDDING CHINCHA STYLE

A very popular dessert of European origin and one richly endowed with eggs, sugar, vanilla, raisins, and walnuts, among other things. One can find bread puddings all over Peru but this version from Chincha is, in my opinion, one of the best.

2	large loaves white bread, about 3 pounds, sliced
3	cups milk
8	eggs, beaten
½	cup sugar for the pudding
¼	cup butter or margarine, well softened
2	teaspoons vanilla
¾	cup raisins
½	cup chopped walnuts
	Grated zest of 1 orange (about 1 tablespoon)
	Grated zest of 1 lemon (about 1 teaspoon)
1½	cups sugar to be caramelized

1. Tear the bread into not-too-small pieces. In a wide bowl soak the bread in the milk, mixing well. Add all the remaining ingredients, except the 1½ cups sugar. Combine well.

2. In a heavy skillet melt the sugar over low heat until caramelized, about 15 to 20 minutes. Quickly pour the caramel into a 9 x 14 inch Pyrex baking dish or pan of similar size and tilt the pan to cover the bottom completely. Allow the caramel to cool and harden for 10 minutes.

3. Now pour the bread mixture into the dish and smooth the top. Bake in a preheated 350 degree oven for 45 minutes. Test the pudding for doneness by plunging a knife or wooden skewer into the center. If it comes out clean, the pudding is done. If not, bake another 5 to 10 minutes. Cool. Turn the pudding out onto a serving platter. Refrigerate until chilled.

Serve cool, cut into 3-inch squares. **Serves 8 to 10**

Mazamorra Morada (Lima)
PURPLE CORN WITH FRUIT DESSERT

This extraordinary sweet is a lightly thickened gelatin with a beautiful purple color that is provided by the pre-Hispanic dried corn. The recipe has historical relevance. The indigenous Indian tribes who existed before and after the Spanish Conquest of Peru lived off the many varieties of corn (choclo), which were unknown to the continents of Europe, Africa, and Asia.

¼	**cup pitted dried prunes**
½	**cup large raisins**
½	**cup dried apricots**
12	**cups (3 quarts) water**
1	**pound dry purple corn, on the cob (see Note)**
1	**cup cubed ripe fresh pineapple (1 inch pieces)**

1	**quince, sliced (optional and seasonal)**
1	**apple, quartered**
1	**cinnamon stick, 3 inches long**
3	**whole cloves**
1	**teaspoon ground anise**
2½	**cups brown sugar**
2	**tablespoons cornstarch dissolved in ¼ cup water**
½	**teaspoon cinnamon**
	Cinnamon, for serving

1. Soak the prunes, raisins, and apricots in water to cover for ½ hour. Drain.

2. Bring the 12 cups water to a boil in a large pan. Add the corn, pineapple, quince (if used), apple, cinnamon stick, cloves, and anise. Simmer over low heat for about 45 minutes, until the purple corn kernels open.

3. Strain the purple corn cooking liquid into a large pan and add the prunes, raisins, apricots, and sugar. Mix well to dissolve the sugar. Discard the cooked purple corn.

4. Add the cornstarch mixture and stir well.

Chill in the refrigerator for several hours. Transfer to a large bowl and dessert will have a loose gelatinous texture; it will not be at all firm.

Serve sprinkled lightly with cinnamon. **Serves 8**

Note: Dry purple corn on the cob is sold in packages in Peruvian grocery stores.

Dulce de Zapallo (Trujillo)

SWEET SQUASH PUDDING

*Zapallo is a giant squash, the largest I have ever encountered
that averages about 24 inches in diameter and can be even bigger. The
eye-catching firm green mottled skin of the zapallo covers an attractive
yellow/orange pulp, which is revealed when the market women cut large
slices of it for avid buyers. "Don't touch," I was cautioned by one, who
explained that the fresh clean color attracted the public.*

4	pounds *zapallo* (see **Glossary**) or butternut squash, peeled and cut into ½-inch cubes
½	cup milk or water
3	whole cloves
¼	teaspoon anise seeds or ground anise
I	cinnamon stick, 3 inches long
I½	cups sugar
2	tablespoons cornmeal dissolved in ¼ cup water
½	teaspoon ground cinnamon, for serving

1. Put the squash, milk or water, cloves, anise, and cinnamon stick in
a large pan and simmer over low heat for 15 minutes. Stirring, add the
sugar and stir for 5 minutes.

2. Stir in the cornmeal mixture and continue to stir for 5 minutes, until
the sweet becomes a purée.

Serve warm or at room temperature, sprinkled with the ground
cinnamon. **Serves 10**

Sango de Trigo (Cuzco)

WHOLE WHEAT RAISIN AND WALNUT PUDDING

An imaginative dessert enjoyed in Cuzco at an elevation of about 10,000 feet. The whole wheat kernels (berries) should be lightly toasted in a nonstick skillet, then ground to a flour, as the people of Cuzco do to prepare them. The richness of this sweet depends upon the spices, raisins, and walnuts, not to mention the aroma of the toasted wheat berries.

8	cups (2 quarts) milk
3	cinnamon sticks, 3 inches each
3	whole cloves
2	to 3 cups whole wheat berries, toasted until the aroma rises
¼	cup sugar
½	cup dark raisins
½	cup walnuts, ground but not too fine, with some texture

1. Bring 6 cups of the milk to a boil over moderate heat in a pan with the cinnamon sticks and cloves. Simmer over low heat for 5 minutes.

2. Grind the toasted wheat berries to a flour in a food processor.

3. Dissolve 2 cups of the flour in the remaining 2 cups cold milk. Add the mixture to the milk and spices, stirring constantly. As it thickens, let it simmer for 15 minutes; add the sugar, raisins, and walnuts.

Pour the mixture into a Pyrex dish and refrigerate. Note that even though this is a soft pudding it is firm enough to slice.

Serve cold, sliced in rectangles. **Serves 8 or more**

Pastel de Choclo (Arequipa)

CORNMEAL CAKE WITH RAISINS

The raisins of Peru are very large and sweet and they melt in this cake, the best I have ever eaten. They make this one of the most delicious sweets in Peru for the coffee or tea hour, or for dessert.

This is a large cake, and I suggest halving the recipe the first time you make it. Bake it in a 9-inch square baking pan.

3½	cups cornmeal
3½	cups flour
5	eggs, lightly beaten
2	tablespoons baking powder
3½	cups fresh milk (not evaporated)
¼	pound butter or margarine, melted
1	cup sugar
½	cup large dark raisins
½	teaspoon ground anise
⅓	cup orange juice
2	tablespoons shredded coconut

1. Mix the cornmeal and flour together. Set aside.

2. In a large bowl combine the eggs and baking powder. Add the 2 flours and milk and mix well. Then add the melted butter and stir to combine thoroughly.

3. Stir in the sugar, raisins, anise, and orange juice, mixing very well. Cover and set aside for 5 minutes.

4. Rub a Pyrex or other baking dish 9 x 12 inches with butter and dust with flour. Pour the batter into the dish and sprinkle the coconut over the top. Bake in a preheated 350 degree oven for ½ hour. Test the old-fashioned way by plunging a wooden skewer into the center. If it comes out dry, then the cake is done. If not, bake the cake another 5 minutes (or more) as the top turns brown. Remove and let cool slightly.

Serve warm or at room temperature. **Serves 6 to 8** (These are large portions, the way the Peruvians like them)

Maicillas (Cuzco)

CORNMEAL AND RUM COOKIES

On the Day of the Dead (November 1), the people of Cuzco visit the cemeteries where their loved ones are buried with offerings of maicillas. These delectable cookies are not for sadness but something to shout about.

- 2 **pounds cornmeal, ground fine**
- 1 **pound lard (recommended by my teacher) or butter or margarine, at room temperature**
- 10 **eggs, separated**
- 1½ **cups sugar**
- ½ **cup pisco (see Glossary) or rum**
- 1 **tablespoon sesame seeds**

1. In a large bowl mix the cornmeal and lard (or other fat) together until blended.

2. Beat the egg whites until frothy. Add the sugar, bit by bit until completely incorporated and the meringue is stiff. Fold into the cornmeal mixture.

3. Beat the egg yolks until light and add them to the batter. Stir in the pisco or rum and incorporate it into the dough. (This is a firm mixture, similar to bread dough.)

4. Form 2-inch balls of the dough. Flatten each until ¼ inch thick, scatter a few sesame seeds on the top, and place on a baking sheet, leaving 2 inches in between. Bake in preheated 400 degree oven for ½ hour. The cookies should be a very light beige—not dark brown. Watch closely! **Makes 25 cookies**

Pecana Relleno (Lambayeque)

STUFFED PECANS

Peruvian agriculture, with a little investigation, surprises. There are extensive orchards of pecans in Peru and the shelled nuts of enormous size are often seen in the public markets. These stuffed pecans, each neatly wrapped in tissue paper, I discovered for sale in a candy shop in Lambayeque. Later in the day I was taught the recipe in that town. They are excellent.

THE WHITE FUDGE (MANJAR BLANCO)

4   cups (1 quart) fresh milk

1   cup sugar

¼   teaspoon baking soda

1   cinnamon stick, 3 inches long

½   teaspoon cornstarch dissolved in
     2 teaspoons cold water

Put all the ingredients in a pan and bring to a boil over moderate heat. Cook for 10 minutes, then reduce the heat to low and simmer for about 1 hour, stirring frequently. When the mixture comes away from the sides of the pan and has the consistency of thick paste, it is ready. Remove from the heat, cool well, and set aside. Remove the cinnamon stick.

THE SUGAR SYRUP (ALMIBAR)

2   cups cold water

1   cup sugar

In a heavy saucepan combine the sugar and water and simmer over low heat for about ½ hour to dissolve the sugar. When the syrup gets to the consistency of honey, it is ready. Remove from the heat, cool, and set aside.

THE STUFFED PECANS

20   large pecan halves

1   cup confectioners' sugar

20   wax or tissue paper squares, each 3½ x 3½ inches

1. Spoon 2 tablespoons white fudge into your palm. Press 1 pecan half in the center. (If the fudge is too sticky, dust with the confectioners' sugar and roll into index-finger-sized pieces, 2½ inches long and ½ inch thick. Make confections with the remaining ingredients in the same way.

2. Cook the stuffed pecans in the sugar syrup for 10 minutes. Remove and let dry on a plate or on wax paper for 10 to 15 minutes. Roll up in the wax or parchment paper squares and twist closed on both ends. **Makes 20**

Dulce de Coco (Lambayeque)

COCONUT BALL SWEETS

½   cup white fudge (Manjar Blanco)

¼   cup desiccated sweetened coconut shreds

Confectioners' sugar, for dusting

Mix the fudge and coconut together and shape into round balls 1 inch in diameter. Roll each generously in the confectioners' sugar.

Store in a jar with a tight cover. **Makes about 16 candies**

Frijol Colado (Callao)

SWEET BLACK BEAN PURÉE

One could add to the title "from grandmother's kitchen" because, according to my teacher, this recipe is about fifty years old and was a popular snack back then in her family.

- **2** cups dried black beans, soaked in water overnight, and drained
- **1** teaspoon ground cinnamon
- **½** teaspoon ground cloves
- **3** cups brown sugar
- **3** tablespoons ground sesame seed
- **1** cup evaporated milk
- **1** tablespoon whole sesame seeds, toasted

1. In a pan cover the beans with water then simmer over low heat until tender, about ½ hour. Drain, reserving 1 cup of the liquid. Purée the beans until smooth.

2. Bring the reserved cup of liquid to a boil in a pan, add the cinnamon, cloves, and the sugar and mix well. Now add the puréed beans, milk, and the ground sesame seeds and simmer, stirring continuously until "you can see the bottom of the pan," or as the puréed beans pull away from the bottom. Let cool slightly.

Serve at room temperature, as a snack anytime, with cookies. **Serves many, at least 10**

PRINCIPALES
DÕIVCAPCHAINDIOTRI
bu rono gran boenacho tiene   que reo yñs ensu pueblo.

uinoanejo

chicha fresca

enes de reyno   don

Chicha o Refresco de Quinua (Saylla)

QUINOA DRINK

*The tiny quinoa seeds have many guises that are known to the
Quechua people of the Cuzco region where Saylla is situated.
This is of an unconventional refreshment that is drunk cold and is not
fermented. It is the drink of the Quechuas of Cuzco.*

- 1   cup quinoa (see Glossary)
- 2   cups dried white corn (choclo)
- ⅔   cup rice
- 16   cups (4 quarts) water
- 3   cinnamon sticks, each 3 inches long
- ¼   teaspoon anise seeds
- 5   whole cloves
- 1   cup sugar, or to taste

1. Grind the quinoa, corn, and rice together into a relatively smooth
flour. Moisten with 2 cups of the water.

2. Bring the balance of the water to a boil in a very large pot over
moderate heat with the cinnamon sticks, anise, and cloves. Add the
ground quinoa mixture and bring to a boil. Boil rapidly for 1 minute.
Pour the mixture through a metal sieve into a large container. Discard
the solids. Refrigerate.

Drink cold. **Serves 10 persons**

Jugo de Quinua con Manzana (Puno)

QUINOA AND APPLE HOT TODDY

The Incas were reputed to live to 100 to 120 years, but then they knew about the virtues of quinoa and its healthful attributes.

I discovered this drink early one morning on All Saint's Day outside the entrance to the Puno central market. The brilliant sun reflecting from Lake Titicaca was, to me, both hot and cold in the rarefied atmosphere. Peasant women wearing polleras—the 3 or 4 underskirts—flounced along carrying huge bundles of flowers for sale. A crowd gathered around the attractive young woman dispensing this hot toddy in glass mugs. The recipe for this old-time traditional drink is as follows.

I	cup dry quinoa (see Glossary)
2½	cups water
I	pound (3 or 4) apples, red or green, sweet or acid
6	whole cloves
I	cinnamon stick, 3 inches long
I	tablespoon sugar, or more to taste
¼	cup cornstarch dissolved in ½ cup cold water

1. Mix the quinoa and 2 cups of the water in a large pan and bring to a boil. Simmer over low heat while you prepare the apples.

2. Peel, quarter, and core the apples. In a food processor process them to a fine purée with the remaining ½ cup water. Add the apple to the quinoa purée with the cloves, cinnamon stick, and sugar and cook for 15 minutes. Add the cornstarch mixture and stir constantly for 5 minutes as the toddy thickens. It should have the consistency of maple syrup but not a thin one. Adjust the sugar should you prefer something on the light sweet side. Remove from the heat.

Serve hot or cold (but hot is better). **Serves 8**

Pisco Sour

*The preeminent alcoholic drink in Peru is pisco sour, which is
prepared from grape brandy, lime juice, and egg white, among other things.
Tourists love it and Peruvians are proud of their brandy, the best ones coming
from the Ica Valley region. The vineyards there were established by early
Italian immigrants and have prospered ever since.*

*I sipped pisco sours (after 5 P.M.) in every city in which I was
doing culinary research. They were all good, but the best ones were in Lima
and Chiclayo, both in Chifa (Chinese) restaurants. My preference was
always the Ocucaje pisco from Ica.*

2   ounces pisco (grape brandy, see above)
1   teaspoon sugar
2   teaspoons fresh lime juice
½   cup crushed ice
1   egg white
     A drop or two of Angostura bitters, or (my choice)
     a shake or two of ground cinnamon

1. Blend together the pisco, sugar, lime juice, and crushed ice. Then add
the egg white and blend it for a few seconds until a thick foam forms.

2. Pour into a wine glass and add either the bitters or cinnamon.

Sip slowly, but with gusto. **Makes 1 drink**

Mate de Coca (All Peru)

Coca tea is produced from the coca leaf, which also produces, after considerable chemical processing, cocaine. However, the similarity ends there since coca tea is not addictive. It is, however, reported to be a cure for altitude sickness, when one comes from sea level to, for example, the 10,000-foot altitude of Cuzco. It was there that I drank coca tea for the first time and as far as I could determine nothing happened that was alarming. The tea also assists digestion, wards off the cold, and perhaps the evil eye. I enjoyed coca tea and had a cup of it almost every day during my tour of Peru.

INDEX

A

A lady from Lima sighs, 242
Abnuerzo de quinoa, 47
Achiote, 7
   aji-chili-spiced shrimp, 91
   barbecued spicy beef hearts on a
     skewer, 122
   classic Peruvian tamales, 14
   steamed whole corn kernel
     tamales, 16-17
Adobo de chancho, 127, 130, 131
Aguadito-salsa de cebolla, 208
Aji, 1, 7
   —de calabaza, 234
   —de camarones, 89
   —de gallina, 169, 172
   classic Peruvian tamales, 14
   fresh corn soup, 43
   steamed whole corn kernel
     tamales, 16-17
   stuffed mashed potatoes, 29
Aji amarillo
   —devilled potatoes with, 227
   —spiced shrimp, 91
   —with shrimp, 89
   alpaca steak stir-fry, 152
   barbecued spicy beef hearts on a
     skewer, 122
   beef fillet with vegetable sauce,
     109
   ceviche Cuzco style, 61

chicken
   in red pepper sauce, 165
   peanuts, and hot chili, 166
   threads with escabeche, 172
chili chicken with walnuts, 169
crisp fried guinea pigs, 154
duck
   and vegetables peasant style,
     185
   stew, 194
everyday table condiment, 206
fish
   chowder at the port, 63
   fry with vegetables, 73
   salad cooked in lime juice, 60
fisherman's soup/stew, 64
fried shrimp with garlic sauce, 92
ground nut condiment, 209
mashed rocotos with garlic, 210
onion and lime juice side dish,
   138
pan-roasted ribs of kid, 147
pickled
   duck salad, 191
   hen with vegetables, 182
pork
   in a spicy sauce with potatoes,
     127
   in wine, 131
potatoes in cheese sauce, 226

roast leg of pork mountain style, 133

shrimp and vegetable stew for Friday, 93

spaghetti and chicken, 179

spicy
chicken salad, 177
sauce, 139

stuffed-Peruvian rocoto, 115

tripe stew of young kid, 150

white cheese sauce, 139

young kid stew, 149

Aji charapa, 206

Aji chili
—devilled potatoes with, 227
—spiced shrimp, 91
—with shrimp, 89
—zapallo stew with, 234
chicken
in red pepper sauce, 165
threads with escabeche, 172
peanuts, and hot chili, 166
chili chicken with walnuts, 169
crisp fried guinea pigs, 154
duck
stew, 194
with rice from Chiclayo, 190
fisherman's soup/stew, 64
fricassee of pork, 134
fried shrimp with garlic sauce, 92
green rice with chicken, 175
guinea pig stew, 155
hot sauce condiment, 207
kid stew with red wine, 148
lamb stew with vegetables, 146
onion and lime juice side dish, 138
pan-roasted ribs of kid, 147
pig's feet in vinegar sauce, 218
pork
and freeze-dried potatoes, 132

in a spicy sauce with potatoes, 127

potato and fresh cheese Chiclayo style, 225

potatoes in cheese sauce, 226

quail eggs and chicken stir-fry, 184

roast leg of pork mountain style, 133

seafood and rice, 99

spaghetti and chicken, 179

special chicken in peanut sauce, 176

spicy
chicken salad, 177
shrimp paste with potatoes, 96
young kid stew, 149

Aji-chili-spiced shrimp, 91

Almibar, 252

Alpaca steak stir-fry, 152

Amazon
fish soup, 67
Shipibo Indians, 66

Anticuchos, 122

Appetizers, 13
crisp fish cubes, 26
crispy
fried mixed seafood, 100
pork cubes, 27
devilled potatoes with yellow aji chili, 227
fresh cheese salad side dish, 215
fried turtle liver, 157
ocopa from Arequipa, 20
pig's feet in vinegar sauce, 218
potatoes
and seaweed, a vegetarian dish, 229
in cheese sauce, 226
stuffed
green mussels, 88

mashed potatoes, 29
squid, 84
Aquadito de pollo, 160
Arequipa
baked custard, 238
boneless stuffed turkey, 198
cheese sauce from a picanteria,
211
cornmeal cake with raisins, 250
crisp fried boneless chicken, 173
fresh cheese salad side dish, 215
lamb, dry roast, 143
mashed rocotos with garlic, 210
ocopa from Arequipa, 20
pig's feet salad side dish, 217
pork in wine, 131
potato pie, 228
salad side dish, 213
with beef, 216
shrimp
and vegetable stew for Friday,
93
in the shell with seaweed, 95
with aji chili, 89
soup of 7 meats, 55
spaghetti and chicken, 179
special freshwater shrimp soup,
40
spicy shrimp paste with potatoes,
96
stew of three meats, 180
stuffed-Peruvian rocoto, 115
zapallo stew with aji chili, 234
Aromatic milk custard, 238
Arroz
—chaufa mixto, 142, 165
—con leche, 244
—con mariscos, 99
—con pato
Chiclayo, 188
Trujillo, 187

—verde con pollo, 175
Asado carne de res, 110

B

Bacalao, 83
Baked
—custard, 238
—spaghetti, 231
—trout in tomato sauce, 86
Barbecued spicy beef hearts on a
skewer, 122
Batido de rocotos, 210
Bean and two-meat stew, 141
Beans and rice, 230
Beef
—and vegetable
pies, 26
soup with wheat kernels, 46
—barbecued spicy hearts on a
skewer, 122
—fillet with vegetable sauce, 109
—pot roast, 110
—salad side dish with, 216
—steak stir-fry, 111
—stew in cilantro sauce, 114
—tongue in tomato sauce, 123
—tripe stew, 119
bean and two-meat stew, 141
boneless stuffed turkey, 198
cow's feet in peanut sauce, 121
creole soup, 44
meat and vegetable boiled dinner,
137
meats at carnival, 118
soup of 7 meats, 55
spaghetti with two meats, 140
special soup with meat, seafood
and vegetables, 56
steak for the poor, 112
stew of three meats, 180
stuffed

Peruvian green gourd, 117
Peruvian rocoto, 115
snacks, 21
Beef, the thickening of Mondays,
    108
Besan, 197
Bijau, 17
Boneless
    —chicken bits with cloud ears,
      161
    —pork
      in tamarind sauce, 128
      in vinegar sauce, 130
    —stuffed turkey, 198
Bread pudding Chincha style, 245
Breast of chicken
    —Italian style, 162
    —rolls, 163
Budin, 245

C

Cabrito chiclayano, 147
Caigua. *see also* Green gourd
    —con relleno
      de pescado, 81
      de pollo, 170
    —fish-stuffed, 81
    —relleno, 117
    —stuffed Peruvian green gourd,
      117
Calamar relleno, 84
Caldo
    —de 7 carnes, 55
    —de carnero, 50
    —de gallina
      estilo Cuzco, 53
      regional, 52
    —de pescado, 67
Callao
    assorted seafood omelet, 103
    breast of chicken

Italian style, 162
rolls, 163
chicken in red pepper sauce, 165
chili chicken with walnuts, 169
devilled potatoes with yellow aji
    chili, 227
fish
    for men, 68
    in onion and tomato sauce, 77
pork and freeze-dried potatoes,
    132
spaghetti in green sauce, 232
steak for the poor, 112
steamed fish fillets, 72
sweet black bean puree, 254
tamarind sauce with pineapple,
    212
Camarones al ajo, 92
Camote, 28
Carapulcra, 132
    —con sopa seca, 166
Cassava, 8. *see also* Yuca
Cau-Cau, 119
Cauche de queso, 211
Causa
    —chiclayana, 73
    —Limena, 29
Cecina, 55
Ceviche, 4, 59
    —Cuzco style, 61
    —de Pescado, 60
    —Japones, 62
    —simple estilo, 61
Chalona, 141
Chancho
    —con salsa tamarindo, 128
    —con tamarindo, 129
Cheese sauce from a picanteria, 211
Cherimoya, 8-9, 243
Chicarrones de chancho de Saylla,
    126

Chicha
—a refresco de quinua, 255
—de jora, 144
Chicharron(es)
—de pollo, 173
—de chancho, 27
—de mariscos, 100
—de pescado, 26
—mixto
Chicken
—and quail eggs stir-fry, 184
—and spaghetti, 179
—boneless bits with cloud ears, 161
—breast
  Italian style, 162
  rolls, 163
—chili with walnuts, 169
—crisp fried boneless, 173
—in red pepper sauce, 165
—peanuts, and hot chili, 166
—rolls in tamarind sauce, 165
—salad side dish with, 216
—soupy with rice, 160
—special in peanut sauce, 176
—spicy salad, 177
—stew, 149
  with red wine, 148
—stuffed caigua, 170
—threads with escabeche, 172
—with green rice, 175
and vegetable pies, 24
barbecued spicy gizzards on a skewer, 123
boneless stuffed turkey, 198
classic Peruvian tamales, 14
dry soup (a pasta), 168
fried rice with assorted meats, 142
hen soup with ground peanuts and cornmeal, 54

meat and vegetable boiled dinner, 137
pickled hen with vegetables, 182
regional soup of the Amazon, 52
rice packages, 19
soup of 7 meats, 55
special soup with meat, seafood and vegetables, 56
steamed whole corn kernel tamales, 17
stew of three meats, 180
stir-fried Japanese style, 181
stuffed mashed potatoes, 30
Chiclayo
aji-chili-spiced shrimp, 91
beef, the thickening of Mondays, 108
chicken threads with escabeche, 172
chili duck with rice, 190
duck
  —and vegetables peasant style, 185
  —with seasoned rice, 188
fish fry with vegetables, 73
fried shrimp with garlic sauce, 92
pan-roasted ribs of kid, 147
pork fry with vegetables, 135
potato and fresh cheese appetizer, 225
shrimp soup, 37
steamed whole corn kernel tamales, 15, 16
tripe stew of young kid, 150
turkey stew in peanut sauce, 196
Chilcano
—de pescado, 63
—de pirana, 42
Chili
chicken with walnuts, 169

duck with rice from Chiclayo, 190

Chincha
assorted stir-fried seafood, 104
bean and two-meat stew, 141
beef
pot roast, 110
stew in cilantro sauce, 114
tripe stew, 119
bread pudding Chincha style, 245
chicken, peanuts, and hot chili, 166
crisp fish cubes, 26
dirty (untidy) custard, 239
dry soup (a pasta), 168
french-fried sweet potato, 28
hot sauce condiment, 207
lamb stew from Chincha, 144
octopus salad, 219
salt fish stew for Easter, 83
simple baked fish, 67
spaghetti with two meats, 140
stuffed
green mussels, 88
squid, 84
zarza, 205

Chinese
boneless pork in tamarind sauce, 128
chicken rolls in tamarind sauce, 165
fish fillets in tamarind sauce, 71

Chirimpico, 150
Choca, 200
Choclo, 61, 246, 255
beef, the thickening of Mondays, 108
Chopped onion condiment dynamite style, 206
Chorizo, 136
Choro a la criallo, 88

Chuno, 9
soup of 7 meats, 55
stew of three meats, 180

Chupe
—de camarones, 37
del mar, 38
del rio, 39, 40
viernes, 93
—de canerejo, 34
—de mariscos de Huanchaco, 102

Coca tea, 259
Coconut ball sweets, 253
Cod. see Corvina
Colapez, 243
Combinado, 114
Condiments
chopped onion dynamite style, 206
everyday table, 206
ground nut, 209
hot sauce, 207
mashed rocotos with garlic, 210
Cooked onion salad, a side dish, 208
Corn leaves, 15-16
Cornish game hens, 199
Cornmeal
—and yuca snacks, 23
—and rum cookies, 251
—cake with raisins, 250
Corvina, 60
fisherman's soup/stew, 63, 64
steamed fish fillets, 72
Cow's feet in peanut sauce, 121
Crab soup, 34
Crayfish. see Freshwater shrimp
Crema Valteada, 240
Creme caramel Peruvian style, 240
Creole
—onion condiment, 204
—soup, 44

Criolla, 1, 165, 177, 215, 218
  boneless pork in vinegar sauce, 130
Crisp
  —fish cubes, 26
  —fried
    boneless chicken, 173
    guinea pigs, 154
 -pork cubes from Saylla, 126
Crispy
  —fried mixed seafood, 100
  —pork cubes, 27
Cuy, 9
  —crisp fried, 154
  —stew, 155
Cuzco
  baked spaghetti, 231
  beef
    and vegetable soup with wheat kernels, 46
    steak stir-fry, 111
    tongue in tomato sauce, 123
  ceviche Cuzco style, 61
  cornmeal and rum cookies, 251
  crisp pork cubes from Saylla, 126
  fava beans, mushrooms, and chinese melange, 221
  fresh corn soup, 43
  ground nut condiment, 209
  hen soup Cuzco style, 53
  lamb and quinoa soup, 49
  mashed sweet potato stuffed with cheese, 28
  meats at carnival, 118
  pickled hen with vegetables, 182
  quinoa soup for lunch, 47
  rabbit stew with peanuts, 156
  roast leg of pork mountain style, 133
  sango de trigo, 249
  wild mushroom melange, 222

D
Deer steak in red sauce, 153
Desserts
  a lady from lima sighs, 242
  aromatic milk custard, 238
  baked custard, 238
  bread pudding Chincha style, 245
  Cherimoya mousse, 243
  coconut ball sweets, 253
  cornmeal
    and rum cookies, 251
    cake with raisins, 250
  creme caramel Peruvian style, 240
  dirty (untidy) custard, 239
  purple corn with fruit, 246
  rice and milk, 244
  sango de trigo, 249
  stuffed pecans, 252
  sweet
    black bean puree, 254
    squash pudding, 248
Devilled potatoes with yellow aji chili, 227
Digados de pato saltado, 195
Dirty (untidy) custard, 239
Dry soup (a pasta), 168
Duck
  —and vegetables peasant style, 185
  —in thick red sauce, 186
  —liver saute, 195
  —pickled salad, 191
  —stew, 194
  —with
    rice, 187
    seasoned rice, 188
  chili with rice from Chiclayo, 190
  soup of 7 meats, 55
Dulce
  —de coco, 253
  —de zapallo, 248

E

Ensalada
 —de pulpo, 219
 - mixta, 214
Escabeche. *see also* Aji
 —de gallina, 182
 —de pato, 191
 —de pollo, 177
Escribano, 213
Espesado
 —de garbanzos, 223
 —de lunes, 108
Estofada de choca, 200
Everyday table condiment, 206

F

Fava beans, mushrooms, and
 Chinese melange, 221
Filet de pescado con salsa de palta,
 75
Fish. *see also* Seafood
 —and plantains, 78
 —crisp cubes, 26
 —fillets
  in tamarind sauce, 71
  Italian style, 70
 —for men, 68
 —fried with avocado puree, 75
 —fry with vegetables, 73
 —garlicked fried, 76
 —head concentrate, 64
 —in onion and tomato sauce, 77
 —layered with vegetables and
  ginger, 79
 —salad cooked in lime juice, 60
 —salted stew for Easter, 83
 —shellfish stir-fry with
  mushrooms, 98
 —simple baked, 67
 —soup, 67
 —steamed fillets, 72

 —stuffed caigua, 81
 and plantain melange, 80
 baked trout in tomato sauce, 86
 broth, 35-37, 56, 91, 93, 98
 ceviche Cuzco style, 61
 crab soup, 34
 fisherman's soup/stew, 64
 freshwater shrimp soup, 39
 fried roe, 88
 green mussel soup, 36
 Peruvian/Japanese ceviche, 62
 piranha broth, 42
 sea shrimp soup, 38
 seafood soup, 41
 shrimp soup, 37
 special
  freshwater shrimp soup, 40
  soup with meat, seafood and
  vegetables, 56
 stuffed
  mashed potatoes, 30
  trout, 87
 yuca packages, 17
Fisherman's soup/stew, 64
French fries, 104, 109, 173
 steak for the poor, 112
French-fried sweet potato, 28
Fresh
 —cheese salad side dish, 215
 —corn soup, 43
Freshwater shrimp, 39, 40
Fricase de chancho, 134
Fricassee of pork, 134
Fried
 —fish
  roe, 88
  with avocado puree, 75
 —rice with assorted meats, 142
 —shrimp with garlic sauce, 92
 —turtle liver, 157
 —vegetable dumplings, 233

Frijol colado, 254
Frito de chancho, 135

G

Gallina enrollado, 163
—con salsa tamarindo, 165
Garlicked fried fish, 76
Goat, 55
Green
—beans, 183
—gourd. *see* Caigua
—mussel soup, 36
—rice with chicken, 175
Ground nut condiment, 209
Guinea pig stew, 155
Guiso
—de pato, 186
—de pichones, 199
—de venado, 153
—del cuy, 155
—del pato, 194

H

Hen soup
—Cuzco style, 53
—with ground peanuts and
cornmeal, 54
Higado de tortuga, 157
Hot sauce condiment, 207
Huacatay, 9, 40
cheese sauce from a picanteria,
211
ocopa from Arequipa, 20
shrimp
in the shell with seaweed, 95
with aji chili, 89
spicy shrimp paste with potatoes,
96
stuffed squid, 84
white cheese sauce, 139
wild mushroom melange, 222

zapallo stew with aji chili, 234
Huanchaco
crispy fried mixed seafood, 100
fried fish roe, 88
potatoes and seaweed, a
vegetarian dish, 229
seafood stew from, 102
Hueveras fritas, 88
Humboldt Current, 59
Humitas, 16, 185

I

Inchicapi de gallina, 54
Iquitos
Amazon Shipibo Indians in, 66
boneless pork in vinegar sauce,
130
chopped onion condiment
dynamite style, 206
cornmeal and yuca snacks, 23
cow's feet in peanut sauce, 121
crispy pork cubes, 27
deer steak in red sauce, 153
everyday table condiment, 206
fish
and plantain melange, 80
and plantains, 78
layered with vegetables and
ginger, 79
freshwater shrimp soup, 39
fried turtle liver, 157
garlicked fried fish, 76
hen soup with ground peanuts
and cornmeal, 54
piranha broth, 42
pork
in tamarind sauce Amazon
style, 129
sausage Amazon style, 136
quail eggs and chicken stir-fry,
184

regional soup of the Amazon, 52
rice packages, 19
roast duck jungle style, 193
yuca packages, 17

J

Japanese
fish broth, 35
fried vegetable dumplings, 233
green mussel soup, 36
seafood soup, 41
shellfish stir-fry with fish and
    mushrooms, 98
special soup with meat, seafood
    and vegetables, 56
Juane, 207
—de arroz, 19
—de Yuca, 17
Jugo de quinua con manzana, 257
Jungle foods
chopped onion condiment
    dynamite style, 206
cornmeal and yuca snacks, 23
deer steak in red sauce, 153
fish and plantain melange, 80
hen soup with ground peanuts
    and cornmeal, 54
rice packages, 19
roast duck, 193
yuca packages, 17

K

Kanigua, 49
Kapche, 221, 222
Kid
—pan-roasted ribs, 147
—stew with red wine, 148
—tripe stew of young, 150
—young, stew, 149

L

Lake Titicaca, 200
Lamb
—and quinoa soup, 49
—dry roast, 143
—stew, 149
    from Chincha, 144
—with vegetables, 146
boneless stuffed turkey, 198
meats at carnival, 118
soup of 7 meats, 55
Lambayeque
aromatic milk custard, 238
assorted mixed vegetable salad,
    214
chicken-stuffed caigua, 170
coconut ball sweets, 253
duck in thick red sauce, 186
fish-stuffed caigua, 81
pigeons in red sauce, 199
puree of zapallo, 234
stuffed pecans, 252
Langousta, 60. *see also* Freshwater
    shrimp
Leche asada, 238
Lengua de res atomatada, 123
Lima
a lady from Lima sighs, 242
cherimoya mousse, 243
fish
    fillets, Italian style, 70
    fish with avocado puree, 75
    rice with assorted meats, 142
pickled duck salad, 191
potatoes in cheese sauce, 226
purple corn with fruit dessert, 246
rice and milk, 244
sea shrimp soup, 38
seafood and rice, 99
stuffed mashed potatoes, 29
young kid stew, 149

Llama, 55
Loma Saltado, 109
Lomo
—a lo pobre, 112
—saltado, 111
Lunches
—quinoa soup for, 47
assorted seafood omelet, 103
fish fry with vegetables, 73
pork in a spicy sauce with
potatoes, 127

M

Maicillas, 251
Mango, 243
Manjar blanco, 238, 252, 253
Marisco saltado con pescado y
hongos, 98
Masa harina, 14
Mashed
—rocotos with garlic, 210
—sweet potato stuffed with
cheese, 28
Mate de coca, 46, 259
Mazamorra
—de cochina, 239
—de pescado con platano, 80
—morada, 246
Meat and vegetable boiled dinner,
137
Meats at carnival, 118
Milanesa
—de pescado, 70
—de pollo, 162
Mondongo, 119
Morqueguano de camaron, 95
Mousse de chirmoya, 243
Mozzarella cheese
chicken and vegetable pies, 25
mashed sweet potato stuffed
with cheese, 28

special freshwater shrimp soup,
40
Mushrooms, 222

O

Ocopa
—Arequipena, 20
—de camarones, 96
Octopus salad, 219
Onion, 208
—and lime juice side dish, 138

P

Paiche
—fish
and plantain melange, 80
and plantains, 78
Pan-roasted ribs of kid, 147
Pango de pescado con platano, 78
Papa
—a la diabla, 227
—a la huancaina estilo
Chiclayano, 225
—de la huancaina, 226
Papa seca, 9, 132
Parihuela peruana, 41
Parrillada de huevo de cordoniz, 184
Pastel
—de choclo, 250
—de papa, 228
Pata de mula, 60
Patita de chancho en fiambre, 218
Patito con mani, 121
Pato
—asado estilo la selva, 193
—saltado a la paisana, 185
Pavo relleno deshuesado, 198
Pebre de tres carnes, 180
Pecana relleno, 252
Pepian
—de conejo, 156

—de pavo, 196
Peppers, 115, 117, 170
   —fish-stuffed, 81
   —mashed rocotos with garlic, 210
Peruvian
   fish broth, 35
   fried vegetable dumplings, 233
   green mussel soup, 36
   shellfish stir-fry with fish and
      mushrooms, 98
   special soup with meat, seafood
      and vegetables, 56
Pescado
   —a lo macho, 68
   —al horno, 67
   —con salsa tamarindo, 71
   —dorado al ajo, 76
   —saute, 72
Peshe de quinoa, 224
Picante de camarones, 911
Picanteria, 1, 9
Pickled
   —duck salad, 191
   —hen with vegetables, 182
Pierna de chancho, 133
Pig's feet
   —in vinegar sauce, 218
   —salad side dish, 217
Pigeons in red sauce, 199
Piranha broth, 42
Pirihuela, 64
Pisco, 251, 258
   tripe stew of young kid, 150
Pizarro, Francisco, 1
Plantains, 80
Plato huanchaquero, 229
Pollo
   —al pimento, 165
   —con yuyo, 161
   —saltado estilo Japones, 181
Pork

—and freeze-dried potatoes, 132
—boneless
   in tamarind sauce, 128
   in vinegar sauce, 130
—crisp cubes, 26
   from Saylla, 126
—crispy cubes, 27
—fricassee of, 134
—fry with vegetables, 135
—in a spicy sauce with potatoes,
   127
—in tamarind sauce Amazon
   style, 129
—in wine, 131
—roast leg of, mountain style,
   133
—sausage Amazon style, 136
bean and two-meat stew, 141
boneless stuffed turkey, 198
fried rice with assorted meats,
   142
meat and vegetable boiled dinner,
   137
pig's feet
   in vinegar sauce, 218
   salad side dish, 217
spaghetti with two meats, 140
whole kernel wheat soup, 51
Potato
—and fresh cheese appetizer
   Chiclayo style, 225
—pie, 228
Potatoes, 2-3, 228
—and seaweed, a vegetarian dish,
   229
—in cheese sauce, 226
—stuffed mashed potatoes, 29
—sweet french-fried, 28
—sweet mashed stuffed with
   cheese, 28
Puchero, 118

Puchucuy de maiz, 23
Puno
  alpaca steak stir-fry, 152
  baked trout in tomato sauce, 86
  chicken and vegetable pies, 24
  cooked onion salad, a side dish,
    208
  fricassee of pork, 134
  prok in a spicy sauce with
    potatoes, 127
  puree of quinoa, 224
  quinoa and apple hot toddy, 257
  soupy chicken with rice, 160
  special chicken in peanut sauce,
    176
  stuffed trout, 87
Puree
  —of garbanzos, 223
  —of quinoa, 224
  —of zapallo, 234

Q
Quail eggs and chicken stir-fry, 184
Queso fresco, 10
  cheese sauce from a picanteria,
    211
  devilled potatoes with yellow aji
    chili, 227
  fava beans, mushrooms, and
    chinese melange, 221
  fresh corn soup, 43
  ocopa from Arequipa, 20
  potato and fresh cheese Chiclayo
    style, 225
  potatoes in cheese sauce, 226
  spaghetti in green sauce, 232
  special chicken in peanut sauce,
    176
  stuffed
    squid, 84
    trout, 87

white cheese sauce, 139
wild mushroom melange, 222
zapallo stew with aji chili, 234
Quinoa, 1, 49. see also Quinon
  —and apple hot toddy, 257
  —and lamb soup, 47
  —drink, 255
  —puree of, 224
Quinon, 10. see also Quinoa

R
Rabbit, 200
  —stew with peanuts, 156
Red onion
  —and tomato side dish, 205
  —salsa, 205
Regional soup of the Amazon, 52
Rice
  —and milk, 244
  —packages, 19
Roast
  —duck jungle style, 193
  —leg of pork mountain style, 133
Rocotos, 115, 210

S
Sajta de pollo, 176
Salad
  —assorted mixed vegetable, 214
  —fresh cheese side dish, 215
  —octopus, 219
  —pig's feet side dish, 217
  —side dish, 213
  —side dish with beef, 216
Salpicon, 216
Salsa
  —con queso, 139
  —criolla, 138, 193, 203, 206
    Zarza, 204
  —de cebolla picada, 206

onion and lime juice side dish, 138

spicy sauce, 139

white cheese sauce, 139

Salso con tamarindo, 212

Salt fish stew for Easter, 83

Salta piquante, 207

—con tomate, 139

Saltado

—de alpaca, 152

—de mariscos, 104

—de pallo, 24

Saltero de queso Zarza, 215

Sancochado criollo, 137

Sango de trigo, 249

Santa Rosa

crab soup, 34

fish chowder at the port, 63

stingray pancake, 85

Sarza red onion condiment, 136

Sauces

cheese from a picanteria, 211

tamarind with pineapple, 212

Saylla, 255

Sazimi peruana, 62

Sea shrimp soup, 38

Seafood, 59. see also Fish

—and rice, 99

—assorted stir-fried, 104

—crispy fried mixed, 100

—omlet, 103

—stew from Huanchaco, 102

aji-chili-spiced shrimp, 91

fish

for men, 68

in onion and tomato sauce, 77

fisherman's soup/stew, 64

fried

rice with assorted meats, 142

shrimp with garlic sauce, 92

octopus salad, 219

shellfish stir-fry with fish and mushrooms, 98

shrimp

and vegetable stew for Friday, 93

in the shell with seaweed, 95

with aji chili, 89

spicy shrimp paste with potatoes, 96

stingray pancake, 85

stuffed

green mussels, 88

squid, 84

Seaweed, 95, 229. see also Yuyo

Seca

—de carne, 114

—de cabrito, 144

Lima, 149

Trujillo, 148

Seco de cordero, 143, 146

Shellfish. see also Seafood

stir-fry with fish and mushrooms, 98

Shipibo Indians, 66

Shrimp

—and vegetable stew for Friday, 93

—broth, 90, 91, 93

—in the shell with seaweed, 95

—soup, 37

—with aji chili, 89

Side dishes

cooked onion salad, 208

onion and lime juice, 138

Sillau, 152

Simple baked fish, 67

Snacks, 13

—stuffed yuca, 21

crisp fish cubes, 26

fish fry with vegetables, 73

mashed sweet potato stuffed
  with cheese, 28
Sopa
—a la criolla, 44
—chambar, 51
—de carnero y quinoa, 49
—de choro, 36
—de frijal, 141
—de maiz, 43
—de trigo, 46
—especial kun fu; 56
—seca, 140, 167, 168
Soup(s), 33. *see also* Stew(s)
—beef and vegetable with wheat
  kernels, 46
—chicken with rice, 160
—crab, 34
—creole, 44
—fish, 67
—fisherman's, 64
—freshwater shrimp, 39
—green mussel, 36
—hen
  Cuzco style, 53
  with ground peanuts and
  cornmeal, 54
—lamb
  and quinoa, 49
  and vegetable, 50
—of 7 meats, 55
—piranha broth, 42
—quinoa for lunch, 47
—regional of the Amazon, 52
—sea shrimp, 38
—seafood, 41
—shrimp, 37
—special
  freshwater shrimp, 40
  with meat, seafood and
  vegetables, 56
—whole kernel wheat, 51

fish broth, 35
sopa de maiz, 43
Soupy chicken with rice, 160
Spaghetti
—and chicken, 179
—in green sauce, 232
—with two meats, 140
Special
—chicken in peanut sauce, 176
—freshwater shrimp soup, 40
—soup with meat, seafood and
  vegetables, 56
Spicy
—chicken salad, 177
—sauce, 139
—shrimp paste with potatoes, 96
Steak for the poor, 112
Steamed fish fillets, 72
Stewed choca, 200
Stew(s). *see also* Soup(s)
—bean and two-meat, 141
—beef
  in cilantro sauce, 114
  tripe, 119
—duck, 194
—guinea pig, 155
—kid with red wine, 148
—lamb
  from Chincha, 144
  with vegetables, 146
—of three meats, 180
—rabbit with peanuts, 156
—seafood from Huanchaco, 102
—shrimp and vegetable for
  Friday, 93
—tripe of young kid, 150
—turkey in peanut sauce, 1966
—young kid, 149
—zapallo with aji chili, 234
Stingray pancake, 85
Stir-fried chicken Japanese style, 181

, 139

nels, 249

egetable soup with,

1

nroom melange, 222

ng kid stew, 149

ca, 10

—and cornmeal snacks, 23

—stuffed snacks, 21

aji-chili-spiced shrimp, 91

beef stew in cilantro sauce, 114

beef, the thickening of Mondays, 108

fish-fry with vegetables, 73

fish salad cooked in lime juice, 60

hen soup with ground peanuts and cornmeal, 54

meats at carnival, 118

packages, 17

pan-roasted ribs of kid, 147

pig's feet in vinegar sauce, 218

pork

   and freeze-dried potatoes, 132

   fry with vegetables, 135

in a spicy sauce with potatoes, 127

regional soup of the Amazon, 52

soup of 7 meats, 55

spicy chicken salad, 177

young kid stew, 149

Yuyo, 161, 229. *see also* seaweed

Z

Zapallo, 10, 40, 46

—puree of, 234

—stew with aji chili, 234

bean and two-meat stew, 141

beef, the thickening of Mondays, 108

duck with seasoned rice, 188

lamb and vegetable soup, 50

meat and vegetable boiled dinner, 137

pan-roasted ribs of kid, 147

shrimp and vegetable stew for Friday, 93

sweet squash pudding, 248

Zapallo stew with aji chili, 234

Zarza, 26, 29, 85, 204, 215-216

—Chincha, 205

—de patitas de chancho, 217

aji-chili-spiced shrimp, 91